Multiple Intelligences

GRADE **1**

teaching kids the way they learn

written by
Sally Cardoza Griffith

Cover by Dawn Devries Sokol
Interior illustrations by Len Ebert and Megan Jeffery
Symbol design by Rose Sheifer

FS-23280 Multiple Intelligences: Teaching Kids the Way They Learn Grade 1
All rights reserved. Printed in the U.S.A.
Copyright © 1999 Frank Schaffer Publications, Inc.
23740 Hawthorne Blvd., Torrance, CA 90505

TABLE of CONTENTS

What Is the Multiple Intelligences Theory?

The Multiple Intelligences Theory, developed and researched by Dr. Howard Gardner, recognizes the multifaceted profile of the human mind. In his book *Frames of Mind* (Basic Books, 1993) Dr. Gardner explains that every human possesses several intelligences in greater or lesser degrees. Each person is born with a unique intelligence profile and uses any or all of these intelligences to acquire knowledge and experience.

At present Gardner has defined eight intelligences. Below are the intelligences and a simplified definition of each. A more complete explanation of each intelligence is found at the end of the introduction.

- verbal-linguistic: word intelligence
- logical-mathematical: number and reasoning intelligence
- visual-spatial: picture intelligence
- musical-rhythmic: music and rhythm intelligence
- bodily-kinesthetic: body intelligence
- interpersonal: social intelligence
- intrapersonal: self intelligence
- naturalist: natural environment intelligence

Gardner stresses that although intelligence is a biological function, it is inseparable from the cultural context in which it exists. He cites the example of Bobby Fischer, the chess champion. In a culture without chess, Fischer would not have been able to become a good chess player.

The Multiple Intelligences Theory in the Classroom

The Multiple Intelligences Theory has been making its way into the educational setting over the past decade. Instinctively, educators have recognized that their students learn differently, respond uniquely to a variety of teaching techniques, and have their individual preferences. Traditional educational programs do not recognize the unique intelligence profile of each student. Traditionally educators have operated according to the belief that there is a single type of intelligence, based on a combination of math and verbal ability. This more one-dimensional view gave rise to the commonly held definition of an "IQ." According to this definition, all individuals are born with this general ability and it does not change with age, training, or experience. Dr. Gardner's theory plays a significant role in rethinking how to educate so as to meet each student's individual needs. Basic skills can be more effectively acquired if all of a student's strengths are involved in the learning process.

The key to lesson design for a multiple intelligences learning environment is to reflect on the concept you want to teach and identify the intelligences that seem most appropriate for communicating the content. At Mountlake Terrace High School in Edmonds, Washington, Eeva Reeder's math students learn about algebraic equations kinesthetically by using the pavement in the school's yard like a giant graph. Using the large, square cement blocks of the pavement, they identify the axes, the X and Y coordinates, and plot themselves as points on the axes.

Other teachers will attempt to engage all eight intelligences in their lessons by using learning centers to focus on different approaches to the same concept. An example of this is Bruce Campbell's third grade classroom in Marysville, Washington. Campbell, a consultant on teaching through multiple intelligences, has designed a unit on Planet Earth that includes seven centers: a building center where students use clay to make models of the earth; a math center; a reading center; a music center where students study unit spelling words while listening to music; an art center using concentric circle patterns; a cooperative learning activity; a writing center titled "Things I would take with me on a journey to the center of the earth."

Another way to use the multiple intelligences theory in the classroom is through student projects. For example, Barbara Hoffman had her third-grade students in Country Day School in Costa Rica develop games in small groups. The students had to determine the objective and rules of the game. They researched questions and answers and designed and assembled a game board and accessories. Many intelligences were engaged through the creation of this project.

Dr. Gardner recommends that schools personalize their programs by providing apprenticeships. These should be designed to allow students to pursue their interests, with an emphasis on acquiring expertise over a period of time. In the Escuela Internacional Valle del Sol in Costa Rica, apprenticeships based on the eight intelligences are used. In one program long-term special subjects are offered to students in areas such as cooking, soccer, and drama. In addition, at the end of the term the entire school participates in a special project in multiage grouping with activities focused around a theme such as Egypt or European medieval life.

Assessment

The multiple intelligences theory challenges us to redefine assessment and see it as an integral part of the learning process. Dr. Gardner believes that many of the intelligences do not lend themselves to being measured by standardized paper and pencil tests. In a classroom structured on the multiple intelligences theory, assessment is integrated with learning and instruction and stimulates further learning. The teacher, the student, and his or her peers are involved in ongoing assessment. In this way the student has a better understanding of his or her strengths and weaknesses. Self-evaluation gives students the opportunity to set goals, to use higher-order thinking skills, as well as to generalize and personalize what they learn.

One example of nontraditional assessment is the development and maintenance of student portfolios, including drafts, sketches, and final products. Both student and teacher choose pieces that illustrate the student's growth. (Gardner calls these *process folios*.) Self-assessment can also include parental assessment, as well as watching videotaped student performances, and students editing or reviewing each other's work.

How to Use This Book

Multiple Intelligences: Teaching Kids the Way They Learn Grade 1 is designed to assist teachers in implementing this theory across the curriculum. This book is for teachers of students in first grade. It is divided into six subject areas: language arts, social studies, mathematics, science, fine arts, and physical education. Each subject area offers a collection of practical, creative ideas for teaching each of the eight intelligences. The book also offers reproducible student worksheets to supplement many of these activities. (A small image of the worksheet can be found next to the activity it supplements. Answers are provided at the end of the book.) Teachers may pick and choose from the various activities to develop a multiple intelligences program that meets their students' needs.

The activities are designed to help the teacher engage all the intelligences during the learning process so that the unique qualities of each student are recognized, encouraged, and cultivated. The activities provide opportunities for students to explore their individual interests and talents while learning the basic knowledge and skills that all must master. Each activity focuses on one intelligence; however, other intelligences will come into play since the intelligences naturally interact with each other.

As a teacher, you have the opportunity to provide a variety of educational experiences that can help students excel in their studies as well as discover new and exciting abilities and strengths within themselves. Your role in the learning process can provide students with an invaluable opportunity to fulfill their potential and enrich their lives.

Words of Advice

The following are some tips to assist you in using the Multiple Intelligences Theory in your classroom.

- Examine your own strengths and weaknesses in each of the intelligences. Call on others to help you expand your lessons to address the entire range of intelligences.
- Spend time in the early weeks of the school year working with your students to evaluate their comfort and proficiency within the various intelligences. Use your knowledge of their strengths to design and implement your teaching strategies.
- Refrain from "pigeonholing" your students into limited areas of intelligence. Realize that a student can grow from an activity that is not stressing his or her dominant intelligence.
- Work on goal-setting with students and help them develop plans to attain their goals.
- Develop a variety of assessment strategies and record-keeping tools.
- Flexibility is essential. The Multiple Intelligences Theory can be applied in a myriad of ways. There is no one right way.

The Eight Intelligences

Below is a brief definition of each of the eight intelligences, along with tips on how to recognize the characteristics of each and how to develop these intelligences in your students.

Verbal-Linguistic Intelligence

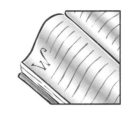

Verbal-linguistic intelligence consists of:

- a sensitivity to semantics—the meaning of words

- a sensitivity to syntax—the order among words

- a sensitivity to phonology—the sounds, rhythms, and inflections of words

- a sensitivity to the different functions of language, including its potential to excite, convince, stimulate, convey information, or please

Verbal-linguistic intelligence consists of the ability to think in words and to use words effectively, whether orally or in writing. The foundation of this intelligence is laid before birth, when the fetus develops hearing while still in the womb. It continues to develop after birth. Authors, poets, newscasters, journalists, public speakers, and playwrights are people who exhibit high degrees of linguistic intelligence.

People who are strongly linguistic like to read, write, tell stories or jokes, and play word games. They enjoy listening to stories or to people talking. They may have a good vocabulary or a good memory for names, places, dates, and trivia. They may spell words accurately and communicate to others effectively. They might also exhibit the ability to learn other languages.

Verbal-linguistic intelligence can be stimulated and developed in the classroom by providing a language rich environment. Classrooms in every subject area should include activities to help students develop a passion for language through speaking, hearing, reading, and examining words. Have students write stories, poems, jokes, letters, or journals. Provide opportunities for impromptu speaking, rapping, debate, storytelling, oral reading, silent reading, choral reading, and oral presentations. Involve students in class discussions and encourage them to ask questions and listen. Invite students to use storyboards, tape recorders, and word processors. Plan field trips to libraries, newspapers, or bookstores. Supply nontraditional materials such as comics and crossword puzzles to interest reluctant students.

Writing, listening, reading, and speaking effectively are key skills. The development of these four parts of linguistic intelligence can have a significant effect on a student's success in learning all subject areas and throughout life.

Logical-Mathematical Intelligence

Logical-mathematical intelligence consists of:

- the ability to use numbers effectively

- the ability to use inductive and deductive reasoning

- the ability to recognize abstract patterns

This intelligence encompasses three broad, interrelated fields: math, science, and logic. It begins when young children confront the physical objects of the world and ends with the understanding of abstract ideas. Throughout this process, a person develops a capacity to discern logical or numerical patterns and to handle long chains of reasoning. Scientists, mathematicians, computer programmers, bankers, accountants, and lawyers exhibit high degrees of logical-mathematical intelligence.

People with well-developed logical-mathematical intelligence like to find patterns and relationships among objects or numbers. They enjoy playing strategy games such as chess or checkers and solving riddles, logical puzzles, or brain teasers. They organize or categorize things and ask questions about how things work. These people easily solve math problems quickly in their heads. They may have a good sense of cause and effect and think on a more abstract or conceptual level.

Logical-mathematical intelligence can be stimulated and developed in the classroom by providing an environment in which students frequently experiment, classify, categorize, and analyze. Have students notice and work with numbers across the curriculum. Provide activities that focus on outlining, analogies, deciphering codes, or finding patterns and relationships.

Most adults use logical-mathematical intelligence in their daily lives to calculate household budgets, to make decisions, and to solve problems. Most professions depend in some way on this intelligence because it encompasses many kinds of thinking. The development of logical-mathematical intelligence benefits all aspects of life.

Bodily-Kinesthetic Intelligence

Bodily-kinesthetic intelligence consists of:

- the ability to control one's body movements to express ideas and feelings
- the capacity to handle objects skillfully, including the use of both fine and gross motor movements
- the ability to learn by movement, interaction, and participation

Bodily-kinesthetic intelligence begins with the control of automatic and voluntary movement and progresses to using the body in highly differentiated ways. The skillful manipulation of one's body or an object requires an acute sense of timing and direction, as well as the ability to transform an intention into action. Examples of people who possess bodily-kinesthetic intelligence are a dancer using his or her body as an object for expressive purposes and a basketball player who manipulates a ball with finesse. This intelligence can be seen in inventors, mechanics, actors, surgeons, swimmers, and artists.

People who are strongly bodily-kinesthetic enjoy working with their hands, have good coordination, and handle tools skillfully. They enjoy taking things apart and putting them back together. They prefer to manipulate objects to solve problems. They move, twitch, tap, or fidget while seated for a long time. They cleverly mimic other's gestures.

Many people find it difficult to understand and retain information that is taught only through their visual and auditory modes. They must manipulate or experience what they learn in order to understand and remember information. Bodily-kinesthetic individuals learn through doing and through multi-sensory experiences.

Bodily-kinesthetic intelligence can be stimulated and developed in the classroom through activities that involve physical movements such as role-playing, drama, mime, charades, dance, sports, and exercise. Have your students put on plays, puppet shows, or dance performances. Provide opportunities for students to manipulate and touch objects through activities such as painting, clay modeling, or building. Plan field trips to the theater, art museum, ballet, craft shows, and parks.

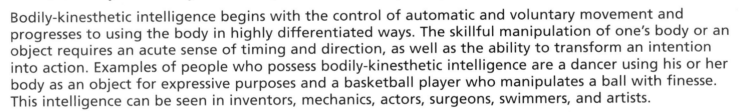

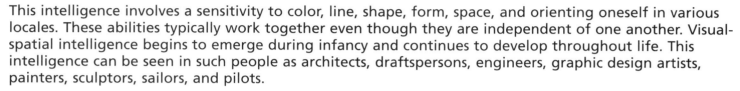

Visual-Spatial Intelligence

Visual-spatial intelligence consists of:

- the ability to perceive the visual-spatial world accurately
- the ability to think in pictures or visual imagery
- the ability to graphically represent visual or spatial ideas
- the ability to orient the body in space

This intelligence involves a sensitivity to color, line, shape, form, space, and orienting oneself in various locales. These abilities typically work together even though they are independent of one another. Visual-spatial intelligence begins to emerge during infancy and continues to develop throughout life. This intelligence can be seen in such people as architects, draftspersons, engineers, graphic design artists, painters, sculptors, sailors, and pilots.

Spatially skilled people enjoy art activities, jigsaw or visual perception puzzles, and mazes. They like to construct three-dimensional models. These people get more out of pictures than words in reading materials. They may excel at reading maps, charts, and diagrams. Also, they may have a good sense of direction.

Visual-spatial intelligence can be stimulated and developed in the classroom by providing a visually rich environment in which students frequently focus on images, pictures, and color. Provide opportunities for reading maps and charts, drawing diagrams and illustrations, constructing models, painting, coloring, and solving puzzles. Play games that require visual memory or spatial acuity. Use guided imagery, pretending, or active imagination exercises to have students solve problems. Use videos, slides, posters, charts, diagrams, telescopes, or color-coded material to teach the content area. Visit art museums, historical buildings, or planetariums.

Visual-spatial intelligence is an object-based intelligence. It functions in the concrete world, the world of objects and their locations. This intelligence underlies all human activity.

Musical Intelligence

Musical intelligence consists of:

- a sensitivity to pitch (melody), rhythm, and timbre (tone)
- an appreciation of musical expressiveness
- an ability to express oneself through music, rhythm, or dance

Dr. Gardner asserts that of all forms of intelligence, the consciousness-altering effect of musical intelligence is probably the greatest because of the impact of music on the state of the brain. He suggests that many individuals who have had frequent exposure to music can manipulate pitch, rhythm, and timbre to participate with some skill in composing, singing, or playing instruments. The early childhood years appear to be the most crucial period for musical growth. This intelligence can be seen in composers, conductors, instrumentalists, singers, and dancers.

Musically skilled people may remember the melodies of songs. They may have a good singing voice and tap rhythmically on a surface. Also, they may unconsciously hum to themselves and may be able to identify when musical notes are off-key. They enjoy singing songs, listening to music, playing an instrument, or attending musical performances.

Musical intelligence can be stimulated and developed in the classroom by providing opportunities to

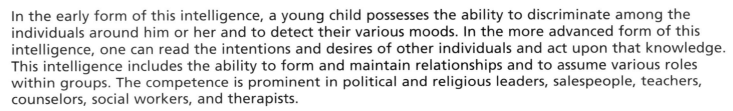

listen to musical recordings, to create and play musical instruments, or to sing and dance. Let students express their feelings or thoughts through using musical instruments, songs, or jingles. Play background music while the students are working. Plan field trips to the symphony, a recording studio, a musical, or an opera.

There are strong connections between music and emotions. By having music in the classroom, a positive emotional environment conducive to learning can be created. Lay the foundations of musical intelligence in your classroom by using music throughout the school day.

Interpersonal Intelligence

Interpersonal intelligence consists of:

- the ability to focus outward to other individuals
- the ability to sense other people's moods, temperaments, motivations, and intentions
- the ability to communicate, cooperate, and collaborate with others

In the early form of this intelligence, a young child possesses the ability to discriminate among the individuals around him or her and to detect their various moods. In the more advanced form of this intelligence, one can read the intentions and desires of other individuals and act upon that knowledge. This intelligence includes the ability to form and maintain relationships and to assume various roles within groups. The competence is prominent in political and religious leaders, salespeople, teachers, counselors, social workers, and therapists.

Interpersonally skilled people have the capacity to influence their peers and often excel at group work, team efforts, and collaborative projects. They enjoy social interaction and are sensitive to the feelings and moods of others. They tend to take leadership roles in activities with friends and often belong to clubs and other organizations.

Interpersonal intelligence can be developed and strengthened through maintaining a warm, accepting, supporting classroom environment. Provide opportunities for students to collaboratively work in groups. Have students peer teach and contribute to group discussions. Involve the students in situations where they have to be active listeners, be aware of other's feelings, motives, and opinions, and show empathy.

The positive development of interpersonal intelligence is an important step toward leading a successful and fulfilling life. Interpersonal intelligence is called upon in our daily lives as we interact with others in our communities, environments, nations, and world.

Intrapersonal Intelligence

Intrapersonal intelligence consists of:

- the ability to look inward to examine one's own thoughts and feelings
- the ability to control one's thoughts and emotions and consciously work with them
- the ability to express one's inner life
- the drive toward self-actualization

This intelligence focuses on the ability to develop a complete model of oneself, including one's desires, goals, anxieties, strengths, and limitations, and also to draw upon that model as a means of understanding and guiding one's behavior. In its basic form, it is the ability to distinguish a feeling of pleasure from one of pain, and to make a determination to either continue or withdraw from a situation based on this feeling. In the more advanced form of this intelligence, one has the ability to detect and to symbolize complex and highly differentiated sets of feelings. Some individuals with strong intrapersonal intelligence are philosophers, spiritual counselors, psychiatrists, and wise elders.

Intrapersonally skilled people are aware of their range of emotions and have a realistic sense of their strengths and weaknesses. They prefer to work independently and often have their own style of living and learning. They are able to accurately express their feelings and have a good sense of self-direction. They possess high self-confidence.

Intrapersonal intelligence can be developed through maintaining a warm, caring, nurturing environment that promotes self-esteem. Offer activities that require independent learning and imagination. During the school day, provide students with quiet time and private places to work and reflect. Provide long-term, meaningful learning projects that allow students to explore their interests and abilities. Encourage students to maintain portfolios and examine and make sense of their work. Involve students in activities that require them to explore their values, beliefs, and feelings.

Intrapersonal intelligence requires a lifetime of living and learning to inwardly know, be, and accept oneself. The classroom is a place where teachers can help students begin this journey of self-knowledge. Developing intrapersonal intelligence has far-reaching effects, since self-knowledge underlies success and fulfillment in life.

Naturalist Intelligence

Naturalist intelligence consists of:

- the ability to understand, appreciate, and enjoy the natural world
- the ability to observe, understand, and organize patterns in the natural environment
- the ability to nurture plants and animals

This intelligence focuses on the ability to recognize and classify the many different organic and inorganic species. Paleontologists, forest rangers, horticulturists, zoologists, and meteorologists exhibit naturalist intelligence.

People who exhibit strength in the naturalist intelligence are very much at home in nature. They enjoy being outdoors, camping, and hiking, as well as studying and learning about animals and plants. They can easily classify and identify various species.

Naturalist intelligence can be developed and strengthened through activities that involve hands-on labs, creating classroom habitats, caring for plants and animals, and classifying and discriminating species. Encourage your students to collect and classify seashells, insects, rocks, or other natural phenomena. Visit a museum of natural history, a university life sciences department, or nature center.

Naturalist intelligence enhances our lives. The more we know about the natural world, and the more we are able to recognize patterns in our environment, the better perspective we have on our role in natural cycles and our place in the universe.

REFERENCES

Armstrong, Thomas. *Multiple Intelligences in the Classroom*. Alexandria, VA: Assoc. for Supervision and Curriculum Development, 1994. A good overview of the Multiple Intelligences Theory and how to explore, introduce, and develop lessons on this theory.

Campbell, Linda, Bruce Campbell, and Dee Dickerson. *Teaching and Learning Through Multiple Intelligences*. Needham Heights, MA: Allyn and Bacon, 1996. An overview and resource of teaching strategies in musical, spatial, bodily-kinesthetic, interpersonal, and intrapersonal intelligences.

Gardner, Howard. *Frames of Mind: The Theory of Multiple Intelligences*. New York: Basic Books, 1993. A detailed analysis and explanation of the Multiple Intelligences Theory.

———. *Multiple Intelligences: The Theory in Practice*. New York: Basic Books, 1993. This book provides a coherent picture of what Gardner and his colleagues have learned about the educational applications of the Multiple Intelligences Theory over the last decade. It provides an overview of the theory and examines its implications for assessment and teaching from preschool to college admissions.

Haggerty, Brian A. *Nurturing Intelligences: A Guide to Multiple Intelligences Theory and Teaching*. Menlo Park, CA: Innovative Learning, Addison-Wesley, 1995. Principles, practical suggestions, and examples for applying the Multiple Intelligences Theory in the classroom. Exercises, problems, and puzzles introduce each of the seven intelligences.

Lazear, David. *Seven Pathways of Learning: Teaching Students and Parents About Multiple Intelligences*. Tucson: Zephyr Press, 1994. Assists in strengthening the child's personal intelligence and in integrating multiple intelligences into everyday life. Includes reproducibles and activities to involve parents.

———. *Seven Ways of Knowing: Teaching for Multiple Intelligences*. Arlington Heights, IL: IRI/SkyLight Training, 1992. A survey of the theory of multiple intelligences with many general activities for awakening and developing the intelligences.

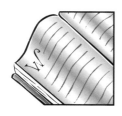

Verbal-Linguistic Intelligence

Race You!

Have children write each of their spelling words for the week on a 1" x 2" strip of tag board. Have them keep the tag board pieces in clean yogurt cups with lids and use them during the week for different activities. One activity to try is a race. Have the children group themselves in pairs. Each person in a pair has a chalkboard, chalk, an eraser, and his or her yogurt cup of words. The children spread their words upside down on the floor. The first person picks up a word, shows it to his or her partner, and reads it aloud. He or she drops it back in the cup, says, "Go!" then both kids race to write the word correctly.

Children can self-check their accuracy by looking at the word in the yogurt cup. If a child misspells the word, he or she should rewrite it correctly. Then, the second person chooses a word, and play continues.

Come for Tea

After children have become very familiar with a story, such as "Goldilocks and the Three Bears," invite two children to have a tea party in front of the class, with each child posing as a character in the story. What would they talk about? Imagine Baby Bear talking to Goldilocks! Be sure to have real cups and saucers as props, and allow children to dress up to help them in their role-playing. This activity is sure to help promote comprehension, as children must be true to their characters and the story. For example, if Baby Bear wants to know why Goldilocks broke his chair, she can't deny it, or say it was broken when she got there!

Me-to-You Mail

After a lesson on question marks and when to use them, open the class computer up to a word-processing program. Invite a child to type a question to another child in the class. That child can type his or her response, then type a question to another child, and so on. Keep the list of questions going—don't erase them! This gives more reading practice for the other children. Remind children, though, that their individual questions will be available for all to see. This way children will get a lot of practice reading, writing, and using question marks.

Logical-Mathematical Intelligence

Comic Strip Stories

In order to demonstrate comprehension of the plot of a story, children can retell the story in comic strip form. The comic strip form uses the four-part sequence: *who, wanted, but, so.* To show students how this works, model the retelling of a story. Using the story "The Three Little Pigs," think out loud:

Who: the wolf.

Wanted: to eat the pigs.

But: he couldn't catch them because they hid in the brick house, which he couldn't blow down.

So: he climbed down the chimney, burned his tail in the pot of boiling water, and jumped out, never to return.

Divide a piece of chart paper into four sections and label them *who, wanted, but,* and *so.* Elicit discussion from the children about what should be written in each section. Next, draw to illustrate each component. Then, using the comic strip you've created, retell the entire story.

Have the children determine the *who, wanted, but,* and *so* features of their stories, then illustrate them in comic strip form using **The Comic Strip** worksheet, which can be found on page 18. Give them ample time to practice retelling their stories before presenting them to the rest of the class.

Color Code It

When children are beginning to write nonfiction, they need help organizing the information they learn. Use the following strategies to help the children organize information. Invite the children to help you as you model the thinking/writing process.

First, brainstorm. Have the children tell you everything they've learned about their subject from books, magazines, videos, and technological research. Use the cluster technique to write down the information they tell you. Write the subject, e.g. bears, in the center of a circle on the board. Draw lines radiating from the circle. At the end of each line, write a sentence, phrase, or word that a child dictates to you.

Next, tell the children that if they were to write a book about what they've learned, it couldn't be mixed up like the cluster; the book would have to be organized. To organize first, examine the information on the cluster. Lead children to discover what questions the information from the cluster answers. Ask them what questions they would expect to be answered in a book about bears.

page 18

Next, write down the questions that the children generate, creating about four broad questions. Number each question and use different colored chalk to write each one. For example: 1. Where do bears live? 2. What do bears do? 3. What do bears eat? 4. What do bears look like?

Then, go back to the cluster. Read each item on the cluster and decide what question it answers. Put an asterisk (*) next to that item using the same color chalk as the question number.

Next, determine in what order the questions should be answered. (In our example perhaps question #4 should be first.) Write down the question order that makes sense to the group.

Finally, look at the color of the first question. On chart paper, write down all the corresponding items marked by that color asterisk from the cluster. Write the items down in a narrative style, not just in a phrase form. Be sure to use a shared writing technique, where you are doing the writing but the children and you are supplying the text. You can also make this an interactive writing activity by inviting the children to write some words on the chart.

After reading, revising, and editing the piece together, the results of your shared writing experience can be typed in large text on the computer, printed, then glued onto several sheets of construction paper. Allow room for illustrations. Hang your big book in your room, or bind it and put it in your class library.

Bodily-Kinesthetic Intelligence

Disappearing Ink

Have the children write their spelling words for the week on 1" x 2" strips of tag board and keep them in clean yogurt containers with lids.

Invite each child to bring his or her yogurt cup, a plastic cup of water, and a clean paintbrush outside on the sunny blacktop or a sunny sidewalk. Have each child take a word out of the container, read it, and put it back in the container. Then have him or her "paint" the word on the ground with water and the brush. Have the children paint each word in capital and small letters. Be sure to have them check the spelling before the word disappears!

What Smells So Good?

Involve the children in sensory descriptive writing by giving them the "popcorn experience." Divide a large sheet of butcher paper into five sections, labeling each section as follows: *Looks, Smells, Sounds, Feels,* and *Tastes.* Bring an air popper; uncooked popcorn; salt; popcorn topping (melted butter or buttery popcorn oil); a big bowl; a large, clean, brown paper grocery bag; and a paper cup for each child.

Gather the children on a rug, put the popper in the middle of the circle, and pop a batch of corn into the big bowl. Invite the children to simply listen and watch. Enjoy their fascination of the process!

When it's finished, pour the popcorn into the paper bag. Repeat the process with a second batch of corn. This time, invite the children to discuss what they see, smell, and hear. Encourage the use of descriptive words and similes. You might say, "Tell me what color you see. What does it look like? What else have you heard that sounds like popcorn popping?" Record their observations on the chart under *Looks, Smells,* and *Sounds.*

Pour the second batch of popcorn into the paper bag, add butter or oil and salt, and serve each child some in a paper cup. Allow the children to sit and eat the popcorn. Encourage conversation about the taste and how the popcorn feels. When everyone has had a few minutes just to enjoy the treat, start eliciting responses for the *Feels* and *Tastes* columns.

When the chart is completed, write a class poem using the following frame. The poem on the right is an example of the activity completed.

I like _____	I like popcorn.
I see _____	I see white flowers.
I smell _____	I smell the movies.
I hear _____	I hear the rain on the roof.
I feel _____	I feel bumpy lumps.
I taste _____	I taste the salty ocean.
I like _____	I like popcorn.

The children can then write their own poems, using the frame of the **My Five Senses Poem** worksheet, provided on page 19.

page 19

Visual-Spatial Intelligence

Bright Words

Set up a learning center where a child can practice his or her spelling words on a Lite-Brite toy. The curved letters won't be perfect, but the visual-spatial learner will enjoy the vivid color and the challenge of making his or her spelling words light up!

Draw What You Hear

Introduce the children to a brand new poem. Choose one that goes with a theme you're currently using, or choose one just because you love it. Copy the poem onto chart paper (without any illustrations). Read it to the children. Invite them to close their eyes and see it with their minds. Encourage them to share their images with each other. What images did their imaginations see? Have them learn and chant the poem together. Then, give each child a printed copy of the poem. Let the children cut out the poems, following the shape of the lines of the text. Have each child glue the poem in his or her poetry journal and illustrate it. Or have each child glue the poem in the center of a large piece of construction paper and draw around the poem.

Tell a Story

Turn off the lights. Light a candle. (If your school doesn't allow candles, use a battery-powered plastic candle—the kind used in windows during the winter holidays.) Drape a shawl around your shoulders and invite the children to listen to you tell a story. Choose a story that you know very well, and be sure to use character voices and great expression.

When finished telling the story, accept your applause. Extinguish the candle and turn on the lights. Invite each child to tell you one thing that he or she enjoyed about your performance and one way that it could be improved. Have the children use "I" statements in their response to you, such as, "I enjoyed the way you used that scary voice when you were the wolf." Or, "I think it would be more interesting if you looked at us more when you talked."

page 20

Map-Maker

Read a story where one character goes somewhere [for example, Red Riding Hood goes to Grandmother's house, or Danny goes to the museum in *Danny and the Dinosaur,* by Syd Hoff (HarperCollins, 1991)]. Invite the children to make a map for the character to use to help him or her get to the destination. Give each child a sheet of white paper. Tell the children that they must include on their maps items found in the story, e.g. the woods, a path, and Grandma's house, in "Little Red Riding Hood," and the museum, the zoo, Danny's house, etc. in *Danny and the Dinosaur.* Have them draw paths, streets, and arrows that show which way the character should go. To provide more intrigue for the visual-spatial learner, children may also complete the maze on the **Which Way Do I Go?** worksheet, found on page 20, which depicts a baby bear going on a search for blueberries. Before handing out the maze, read *Blueberries for Sal,* by Robert McCloskey (Puffin, 1976) to the class.

Musical Intelligence

Read It/Sing It!

Choose a song that the children love to sing. Make a big book of the song by simply typing the text in large print on the computer (or writing by hand), and gluing the text to the bottom halves of 12" x 18" pieces of construction paper. Give the children the opportunity to illustrate the text. Hang the book from a clothesline strung across your room. Children can use pointers to point to the words as they sing and read!

It Sounds Scary!

Distribute rhythm sticks to your children. Read *The Gunnywolf,* by Antoinette Delaney (HarperCollins, 1992). As you read, invite the children to play their sticks according to the tempo of the story. You might lead them by tapping your leg as you read.

Create Your Own Mood

Find music to match the mood of your story. For example, as you're reading *Everybody Needs a Rock,* by Byrd Baylor (Scribner, 1974), play Native American music softly. If you're reading *Leprechauns Never Lie,* by Lorna Balian (Humbug Books, 1994), play some Celtic music softly. Whenever you read about Abe Lincoln, George Washington, Martin Luther King, Jr., or other American political figures, play a patriotic song, such as "America, the Beautiful."

Use music to create an upbeat mood when children walk into the room on a dull, dreary day. Tape record the theme songs from their favorite TV shows and see their eyes light up as they hear them! To quiet down restless children, play classical music such as Bach's Brandenburg Concertos. When children are finishing up work and the mood is full of hustle and bustle, play soundtracks from musicals and sing along!

Interpersonal Intelligence

Pizza Parlor

Read *Little Nino's Pizzeria,* by Karen Barbour (Harcourt Brace Jovanovich, 1990). Set up a dramatic play center with modeling clay, cookie sheets, aprons, pads of paper, pens, a play cash register, and utensils. Invite the children to create their own pizzeria. Children can be cooks, waiters, or customers. You might even have a play phone for take-out orders. Using chart paper, make a menu board with prices. Children will practice reading and writing when ordering and can even practice math if you make the price list appropriate to their skill levels.

Compound Creations

Introduce the concept of compound words to your children. To kick off your compound lesson, read *Blueberries for Sal,* by Robert McCloskey (Puffin, 1976), *The Little Mouse, the Red Ripe Strawberry and the Big Hungry Bear,* by Don Wood (Child's Play, 1990), and *Pancakes, Pancakes,* by Eric Carle (Scholastic, 1992).

Group the children into pairs. Give each pair one of the **Compound Creations** worksheet, found on page 21. Have each child cut out the cards. Have the pairs work to match words from each set to make compound words. They can glue the words together on another sheet of paper, and then write the words.

Name_____
Compound Creations
Work with a partner. Cut out both sets of words. Put the words together to make big words. Write the new words on a piece of paper.

blue	cake
pan	ball
ear	man
foot	berry
fire	ring

page 21

Intrapersonal Intelligence

Free Write

To develop fluency in the children's writing and to connect them to their inner voices, encourage them to write without stopping for ten minutes. Tell the children it is important that they don't stop writing even if they have to write the same word or letter over and over until they think of something else to write. To begin, play classical music softly. Instruct the children to be very quiet so they won't disturb each other's thoughts, and let them write. You might have them write about their feelings about a story you read, how they feel about a certain issue in the classroom, or anything they want. Some children will be at the developmental level where all they can write are strings of letters. Some will stop and struggle over spellings. Coax them to write as much as they can. This is not an activity to edit spellings; make this clear to the students. The important thing is that the children keep writing for the full ten minutes to experience the flow of writing.

Journals

To continue the development of fluency in writing, provide each child with a journal. A journal can be as simple as a piece of folded construction paper with blank pages stapled inside. Provide the children with time to reflect and have them write often in their journals. In September, it is common for first grade journals to be filled with pictures. As the children learn more about writing, their journals become filled with letters, then simple words, as well as pictures. By January, several students may be writing sentences. Encourage fluency by responding to their journal entries with questions such as, "What happened then?" or "How did that make you feel?"

Naturalist Intelligence

Posters for Pet & Plant Care

Allow the naturalists in your room to make posters on how to care for the pets or plants in your classroom. These posters are great aids for substitute teachers, who may otherwise leave your class wondering, "Should I have fed that hamster today?" The posters should say which days of the week the pets should be fed and the plants watered, as well as the amount of food or water to be given. Perhaps instructions on when cages should be cleaned or where supplies are kept in the classroom would be helpful, as well.

Kapok Capers

Read *The Great Kapok Tree: A Tale of the Amazon Rain Forest*, by Lynne Cherry (Harcourt Brace Jovanovich, 1990). Discuss with the children what personal connections they made with the text. Ask them how this story is relevant to each person who hears it.

Make a chart that says, *Why the Man Should Cut the Tree,* and *Why the Man Shouldn't Cut the Tree.* Engage the children in a lively debate. Write their responses on the chart. Then ask them what they would do if they were the man in the story and why.

Name_____

The Comic Strip

Draw pictures to tell a story.

Who	Wanted

But	So

reproducible

FS23280 · Multiple Intelligences Grade 1

LANGUAGE ARTS
Logical-Mathematical Intelligence

My Five Senses Poem

Fill in the blanks to make your own poem. Give your poem a title too.

_____

I like _____.

I see _____.

I smell _____.

I hear _____.

I feel _____.

I taste _____.

I like _____.

LANGUAGE ARTS
Bodily-Kinesthetic Intelligence

Which Way Do I Go?

Help the bear find the berry bush. Draw a line from the bear to the bush.

LANGUAGE ARTS
Visual-Spatial Intelligence

Compound Creations

Work with a partner. Cut out both sets of words. Put the words together to make big words. Write the new words on a piece of paper.

blue	cake
pan	ball
ear	man
foot	berry
fire	ring

LANGUAGE ARTS
Interpersonal Intelligence

Verbal-Linguistic Intelligence

Make a Mini-book

Read Mercer Mayer's *All By Myself* (Western, 1985). Have the children brainstorm all the things they can do by themselves now that they're in the first grade. Make several copies for each child of the **All by Myself** worksheet on page 29 so that children can make their own mini-books of things they can do by themselves. Have them read their books to each other. Make a list of things that your students can do. Review this list with your students. Then discuss and write down the things that the children want to learn to do by the end of the first grade. They can add pages to the book as they accomplish these things.

Name_____

All by Myself

Make your own book about things that you can do all by yourself. Complete the sentence on each page. Draw pictures to match your words. Cut the pages on the dotted lines. Then staple them together to make a book.

| I can ___ all by myself. | **All by Myself** |
| I can ___ all by myself. | I can ___ all by myself. |

page 29

Community Helpers and Effective Listening

Invite a firefighter, dentist, nurse, police officer, or other community helper to your classroom. Before the visitor arrives, make a class chart with the headings *What We Know* and *What We Want to Know* about the visitor's occupation. Have each child prepare a specific question to ask the visitor. Tell children to listen carefully when the visitor speaks. Teach them that often their questions may be answered by the visitor when he or she talks about his or her job. If a child's question has already been answered, they don't need to ask it during the question and answer time.

Invite children to listen as well for one thing that the visitor says that really makes them think, "Aha! I would love this job" or, "Yikes! I would not love this job!" After the visitor leaves, cluster all the information that the children learned on chart paper. Make a new column on the class chart titled *What We Learned*. After filling out this column as a class, have the children use the ideas in the column to write individual thank you notes to the visitor. Visitors will probably be very interested in knowing what was learned by their presentations, and would probably be amused at any comments the children care to share as well.

My Family and Me

Explain to the children that we are all part of a family, and that families are made up of different people. Have each child fill out the **All About Me** worksheet on page 30. Then have each child take home the **For a Family Member** worksheet on page 31 and interview a family member. Ask the children if they learned anything new about the person they interviewed.

Logical-Mathematical Intelligence

It's Logical

Invite the children to present real problems that they notice in their neighborhood or at school. Discuss how some problems can be solved with simple, logical solutions. However, sometimes we don't see the solutions unless they're written down in black and white.

Make a class chart that is divided into three sections: *Problem, Solution,* and *How to Prevent It.* Invite a child to write a problem on the chart (for example, trash on the school ground). Elicit the logical solution to the problem from the children (pick up the trash). Have the children then discuss how to prevent the problem from happening again (put more trash cans around the school).

Who Helps Whom and How?

To really solidify the idea that community helpers are workers who help the people who live in a community, make a class chart using the headings below. Get input from the children to fill out the chart.

Community Helpers	What do they do?	Whom do they help?	How do they help?
Mail Carriers	bring our mail	us	We can receive mail from all over the world.
Police Officers	arrest bad guys	us	They keep us safe.
Nurses	give us shots	us	They keep us well.
Trash Carriers	take our trash	us	They help us keep our homes clean.

Discuss with the children the pattern and relationships developed between community helpers and the people they help—us. Then discuss how we could help make community helpers' jobs easier.

page 30

page 31

Bodily-Kinesthetic Intelligence

Where I Live Chant

Teach the children the following chant so that they learn the relationships between home, city, state, and country. Invite the children to stand up and clap to the beat!

Where I Live

I know my address. (Clap to the beat.)

It's home I love best.

I live at: _____. (Child whispers number and street name.)

I live in a city.

It's really quite pretty.

I live in: _____. (Child says name of city.)

I live in a state.

That's really quite great.

It's name is: _____. (Child loudly declares name of state.)

I live in a country.

Where people are born free.

It's name is: _____. (Child SHOUTS name of country.)

I know where I live.

I know who I am.

I am _____. (Child flings out arms and shouts his or her name.)

and I am HERE! (Child points dramatically to the floor.)

Dress for the Weather Game

Gather two piles of winter clothes (boots, mittens, scarves, hats). Divide the children into two teams. Have the teams form two single lines, one in front of each pile of clothes.

When you call out, "cold hands," the first two children in line race to put on the mittens. Once the mittens are on, they run to the end of the line. Then call out, "wet feet," and the next two children race to put on the boots. Once the boots are on, they run to the end of the line. Continue to call out various cold body parts until the clothes are used up. Then, reverse the process. When you call out, "hot head," the children with the hats run to the front of the lines, take off the hats, and return to the line. Call out, "dry feet!" The children with the boots run to the front, take off the boots, and return to the line.

This game can also be played as a Dress for Summer game. Simply change the piles of clothes to big, old bathing suits, towels, flippers, etc. Call out things like, "What should I wear to swim in?" or "Need to dry off!"

Visual-Spatial Intelligence

Easy Puzzle

On a large poster board, draw the outline of your state with black marker. Cut the state out, and then cut it into several jigsaw pieces. Children can put the puzzle together and learn the shape of their state.

Build a Community

After studying the community, have the children build their own communities. Give each child half a sheet of tag board. Tell the children to figure out which buildings they want in their communities—a hospital, supermarket, post office? Have the children draw x's on the tag board that suggest where they want their buildings. Children can paint empty milk cartons (saved from the cafeteria) for the buildings. Have them staple the tops of the cartons back together to make roofs. Then have them glue the bottom of the milk cartons to the tag board base. Children can use markers or crayons to draw roads between the buildings. They can paint or draw grass. They can use construction paper scraps to make lakes or parks. Have the children name their cities and make "Welcome to ____" signs. Ask the children to decide what makes each city so special. Have them explain why a person would want to live there.

Musical Intelligence

America, the Beautiful

Teach the children to sing "America, the Beautiful." This song lends itself to a big book beautifully! Print the text across the bottom of a long piece of white butcher paper.

Discuss with the children what kinds of pictures they will need to paint so that the pictures match the words. Have them paint a mural across the top part of the butcher paper. One portion could be purple mountains; one could be amber waves of grain. Have the children paint the ocean on the extreme left and right of the butcher paper mural. Label the left side Pacific and the right side Atlantic.

President's Day

Celebrate President's Day with a parade! Have the children dress in red, white, and blue. Make dandy drums by painting oatmeal boxes with red, white, and blue stripes and sticking gummed stars on them. Cut out construction paper stars and tape them to the children's shirts. Using a portable tape recorder, have the children march around the room or out the door into the corridors clapping or drumming their drums as they sing "Yankee Doodle" or "You're a Grand Old Flag."

Interpersonal Intelligence

Celebrations and Traditions

Honor the children's different celebrations (Christmas, Hanukkah, birthdays, etc.) by allowing them to share their families' traditions on these special days. Make construction paper copies (one for each child) of the **My Traditions Star** on page 32. Have each child write the name of his or her holiday/celebration in the middle of the star. On the lines around the star, have the child write words or phrases that capture the essence of his or her family's tradition. For example, in the middle of the star a child might write *My Birthday, January 28*. On the lines of the star, he or she might write, *chocolate cake, Grandma's house, big present, pinata,* and *play with cousins*. If the child wants, he or she can bring a photograph from home that shows the family's celebration. Have the child tape it to the back of the star, punch a hole in the top, and string a piece of yarn through it. Hang it in your classroom. Be sure to allow each child the time to share his or her star with the class and explain about his or her own experiences.

Circle Time

About three times a week, gather the children in a circle. Instruct each child to say something that he or she appreciates about someone else in the classroom. A child may start the statement by saying, "I appreciate the way that___." He or she might say, "I appreciate the way that Jane helped me clean up the paint that I spilled." Tell the children to be on the lookout for someone who treated them with kindness and thoughtfulness. It takes practice, but doing this sets the tone for a gentle classroom.

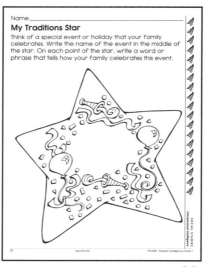

Name_____
My Traditions Star
Think of a special event or holiday that your family celebrates. Write the name of the event in the middle of the star. On each point of the star, write a word or phrase that tells how your family celebrates this event.

page 32

Intrapersonal Intelligence

My Banner

Teach the children that the flag is a symbol that represents our country. Invite the children to design a flag that would represent themselves. What would be on that flag? Have the children think about their favorite sport, color, food, toy, book, place to go, etc. They should use pieces of scratch paper to jot down their ideas. A child might draw a soccer ball, a pizza, a video game, and color the flag purple. Give each child a copy of worksheet page 33, **My Flag.** Have the children draw, color, and cut out their flags. Photocopy your class picture and give each child a picture of himself or herself, which he or she can cut out and glue onto the star on top of the flag pole. Display the flags on a bulletin board titled, "Star-Spangled Banners!" Allow the children to guess whose flag is whose by covering up the pictures of the children with index cards. How well do they know their classmates? You might say, "Which child in Room 7 likes pizza, the color purple, soccer, and video games?" After the children have guessed, uncover the star and see if they're correct.

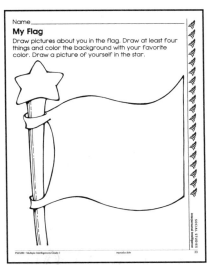

page 33

Make a Class Book—When I Grow Up

Read Mercer Mayer's *When I Get Bigger* (Western, 1985) to the children. Invite them to think about what they will do when they get bigger. Be sure to elicit discussion as to why a child wants to do a certain thing. Make a class book with each child making a page. Use the sentence frame, *When I grow up, I _____* or *When I get bigger, I_____.* Make a construction paper cover and staple or bind the pages together. Read the book to the children, and keep it in the class library for the children to read.

Acrostic Poetry

An acrostic poem begins with one word, such as a child's name. The word is written vertically and each letter of the word is used as the first letter of a sentence, a phrase, or a word that describes the subject or relates to it. Invite the children to write an acrostic poem. Allow them to use the name of a community helper, the name of the city or state in which they live, the name of their school, or the name of themselves or someone in their family.

For example:

Nice and friendly

Usually wears white

Races to help sick people

Stands all day

Extra hard worker

Children will need to see several modeled lessons. You might want to build a list of words that begin with vowels, as they tend to be difficult for children.

Naturalist Intelligence

A Community at Work

Just how well will children organize themselves and get a job done, if we as teachers stand back and leave them alone? Here's an opportunity to find out.

Save the seeds from your Halloween jack-o'-lantern. Wash them and allow them to dry. Store them in a baggie until spring.

When it's springtime tell the children they will plant their very own jack-o'-lantern. Demonstrate how to plant the seeds: Use a clear plastic cup. Write your name on a piece of masking tape with a pencil or pen; press the tape on the cup. Using a tablespoon, fill the cup 2/3 full with potting soil. Press 2 seeds about 1/2 inch below the soil. Water the seeds. Place them on a tray outside in the sunshine.

Next comes the tricky part. Pass out the items needed to plant the seeds to different individuals. For example, two children can each get half the cups. Another child can get one roll of tape. Another can get the bag of potting soil. Tell the children that their seeds need to be planted and the room must be spotless before lunchtime. Then take out a clipboard and pencil and remove yourself to a distant chair, telling the children you have important work to do and to please continue with the planting just as farmers would. What will happen? Will your community share, problem solve, and get the seeds planted? Be sure to discuss the problem-solving strategies used to plant the seeds–or lack of strategy used and ways to work better together next time–at the end of the session.

Equipment needed:

pumpkin seeds

clear plastic cups

masking tape

pencil or pen

tablespoon

potting soil

watering cans

Name_____

All by Myself

Make your own book about things that you can do all by yourself. Complete the sentence on each page. Draw pictures to match your words. Cut the pages on the lines. Then staple them together to make a book.

I can

_____

all by myself.

All by Myself

I can

_____

all by myself.

I can

_____

all by myself.

SOCIAL STUDIES

Verbal-Linguistic Intelligence

Name Harini

All About Me

Write your answers on the lines.
Then draw a picture of yourself
in the frame.

1. What are your favorite foods?

pasta, noodles, pizza and Dosa.

2. What are your favorite sports?

basketball.

3. What is your favorite color?

pink.

4. What are your favorite things to do?

Draw, play and go to party's.

5. What are your least favorite things to do?

I don't like to play with someone who's mean.

6. Which season do you like the best? Why? I like spring

spring

because it's warm.

Name _Harini_

For a Family Member

Ask someone in your family these questions. Then draw a picture of the person. Write his or her name in the space below the picture.

Pushpa

1. What are your favorite foods?

   Briani, sweetchapthi, Biscuit.

2. What are your favorite sports?

   Ring.

3. What is your favorite color?

   Magenta.

4. What are your favorite things to do?

   going to libarry, going walks and Drawing.

5. What are your least favorite things to do?

   I don't like to jump in the trampoline

6. Which season do you like the best? Why? _I like summer beacause its nice and warm._

My Traditions Star

Think of a special event or holiday that your family celebrates. Write the name of the event in the middle of the star. On each line of the star, write a word or phrase that tells how your family celebrates this event.

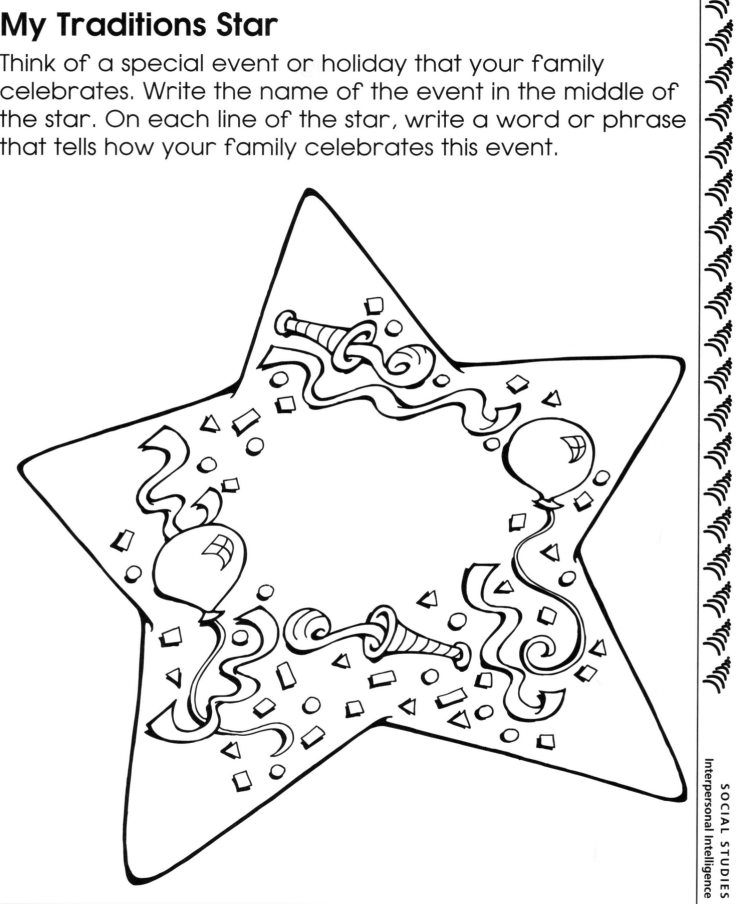

reproducible

SOCIAL STUDIES
Interpersonal Intelligence

My Flag

Draw pictures about you in the flag. Draw at least four things and color the background with your favorite color. Put a picture of yourself in the star.

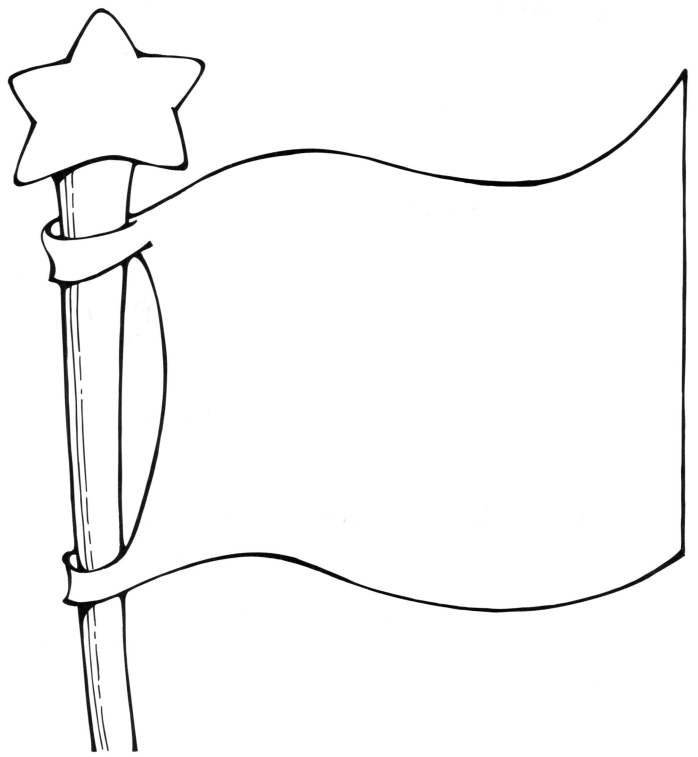

reproducible

SOCIAL STUDIES
Intrapersonal Intelligence

Verbal-Linguistic Intelligence

Math with Mother Goose

Teach the children the number words through the use of this nursery rhyme:

> One, two, buckle my shoe.
>
> Three, four, shut the door.
>
> Five, six, pick up sticks.
>
> Seven, eight, lay them straight.
>
> Nine, ten, the big fat hen.
>
> Sounds pretty good, let's do it again!

Write each line on the bottom half of a 12" x 18" piece of construction paper. (You will need six pieces of paper.) Allow the children to illustrate the rhyme using the top halves of the paper. Hang the pieces of paper up in your classroom. Give the children some interesting addition or subtraction problems, using number words instead of numerals (e.g., six + four = _____). Encourage them to use the nursery rhyme posters to assist them if they have difficulty reading the numbers.

Big Numbers

Ask the children to tell you the largest number that they know. Invite them to write that number down in numerals. (You will get a great variety of responses!) The concept of a million is difficult even for adults to grasp. To capture and stretch your children's imaginations and to help them develop the concept of what a million is, read *How Much Is a Million?* by David M. Schwartz (Scholastic, 1987), and *Millions of Cats,* by Wanda Gag (Putnam, 1996).

Story Problems

Get your children off to a good start with story problems. Give each child a copy of the **Story Problems** worksheet on page 41. Read the first problem together. Have the children underline the question. Reread the problem and have the children circle the numbers that tell how many. Discuss with the class whether addition or subtraction should be used. Have the

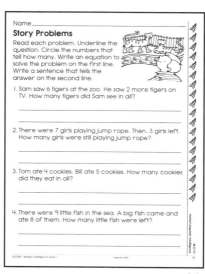

page 41

children write the equation and draw a picture, if necessary. Have the children solve the equation and then write a sentence to tell what the answer is. They should then reread the problem and the answer out loud in a strong voice. Ask them if their answer matches the question—does their answer make sense? Continue this step-by-step model with the children until they feel confident to attempt some problems on their own.

Logical-Mathematical Intelligence

One More

Children need to learn that mathematics contains many patterns. One pattern that might help them to understand and to learn addition facts is: When one more is added to an addend, one more is added to the sum. For example, if $3 + 3 = 6$, then $3 + 4 = 7$. Model this strategy using the logical language *if, then*. You might want to build a chart on butcher paper, where one equation is written directly under the other, so that the children notice the increasing order of numbers:

If: $3 + 3 = 6$,

then: $3 + 4 = 7$.

After directly teaching the students this strategy, have them try the **One More** worksheet on page 42, where they need to fill in missing addends and/or sums.

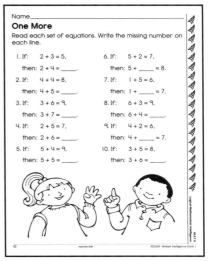

page 42

Counting by Twos, Fives, and Tens.

First grade students need a lot of practice in skip-counting. To help them see the pattern in what they say, give each student a copy of the worksheet on page 43, **"See" What You Count.** The children's first job is to write the numbers from 1 to 100 on the grid. Next, have the children count by twos and color each square that they count yellow. Then have the children count by fives and color each square that they count red. They will notice that they are coloring over some of the yellow squares, making them orange. The orange squares are the groups of five that are also groups of two—the tens. Next, have the children count by tens and outline the box of each number they count with a blue crayon. Gather the children together to discuss the patterns that they notice. Count aloud by twos, fives, and tens as the children use their worksheets to assist them. Also, be sure to count backward by twos, fives, and tens.

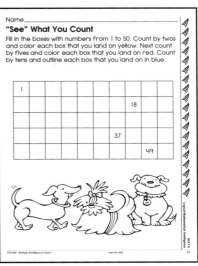

page 43

Bodily-Kinesthetic Intelligence

Grab the Gold!

For a fun way to practice addition and subtraction facts, play "Grab the Gold!" Divide the children up into two teams—the Pirates and the Leprechauns. Have each team stand facing each other in long lines about 20 feet apart. (If possible, it's easy to have them stand on the painted lines of an outdoor basketball court.)

Give each member on the Pirates team an index card with a number from 0–10. Each player must have a different number. (If you have more than 22 children, you'll need to make numbers from 0–11 or 12 or until everyone has a number.) Give the members on the Leprechauns team an identical set of cards.

Draw an X with chalk at a point midway between the two teams. Set a chalkboard eraser (the gold) on the X. Stand on the sidelines and call out an equation (using flash cards makes it easy), such as, "9 minus 6!" The children may have to calculate. Allow them to help each other, if necessary.

The child who has the 3 card from each team runs to grab the gold, the object being to bring the gold to his home team. If one child grabs the gold first, the other child chases him and tries to tag him. If he or she is tagged, the gold is returned to the X and no team gets a point. If, however, a child grabs the gold and returns to his home team without being tagged, his or her team gets a point. A child may be tagged only if he or she is holding the gold. If both children grab the gold simultaneously, the gold "turns to dust," and the players return to their home teams.

When both children have returned to their home teams, call out another equation. An easy way to keep score is to write the points on the blacktop with a large piece of chalk.

Over/Under

To practice counting by ones or to practice skip-counting by twos, fives, or tens, play Over/Under. Divide the class into two teams. Have the teams stand in two lines where children look at the back of the head in front of them. Give each child in the front of a line a beanbag. Call out the "chant" for that race. ("Count by twos to 50.") The first children in line pass the beanbags over their heads to the people behind them as they call out "2!" The persons receiving the beanbags pass them between their legs to the people behind them and call out "4." The beanbags are passed, over and under, as each child continues to count by twos. When the end of the line is reached, the last child runs to the front and continues with the chant, passing the beanbag over his or her head. The first team to reach 50 correctly wins. If someone miscounts, the beanbag "freezes" in his or her hands, until he or she says the correct number (he or she can be coached by the team.)

Count Your Eggs

The game Count Your Eggs is intended to help children understand how numbers can be broken down into groups of tens and ones (for example, 36 is three groups of ten and six ones).

You will need many empty 12-count egg cartons. Cut off the lid and two end egg spaces in each carton. Give each child, or each pair of children, several egg cartons, a small bowl, and access to manipulatives, such as one-inch interlocking cubes, counting bears, or wooden cubes. (Do not use beans.)

Have each child, or each pair of children, scoop up a bowlful of manipulatives. Have the children consider this a "basket of eggs." Next, have the children put each "egg" in an egg space in a carton. When one carton is full, instruct the children to fill another. The children are building groups of ten in the cartons; any extra eggs are left in the basket. When finished, have the children count the cartons and the extra eggs. They might say, "We have 4 cartons of eggs and 2 extra. We have 4 groups of ten and 2 extra. We have 42 eggs!"

Meet Your Feet!

Read *The Foot Book*, by Dr. Seuss (Random House, 1968), to the children. On different colored sheets of 9" x 12" construction paper, have each child trace around one of his or her feet. Then have the child cut out the paper foot. Working in small groups, have each child measure the length of his or her foot from toe to heel with a nonstandard measure, such as interlocking cubes or large paper clips (everyone must use the same instrument to measure). Have them write the number of cubes or clips on the back of each paper foot. Have the children compare their feet. Who has the smallest foot? Who has the largest? Does anyone have feet that are exactly the same size? Encourage the children to use the numbers on the back of the feet to verify what they learn. For example, if a child discovers his or her paper foot is larger than a friend's, have them both check the numbers on the back of the feet. They will see that 7 cubes is more than 5 cubes.

Tape or staple all of the feet around the room at a child's eye level. Invite the children to measure their friends' feet using various nonstandard instruments of measure. You might put up bulletin board letters that say, "Meet Our Feet!"

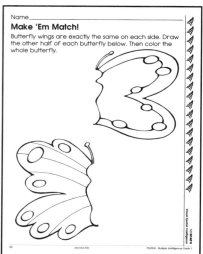

page 44

Name_____

Make 'Em Match!

Butterfly wings are exactly the same on each side. Draw
the other half of each butterfly below. Then color the
whole butterfly.

Visual-Spatial Intelligence

Symmetry

Teach the children that when things are symmetrical, they can be divided along their line of symmetry into two pieces that are exactly alike. Cut a length of string, and invite a volunteer to the front of the room. Hold the string from the child's forehead, down the nose, to the end of the chin. (While faces are not exactly alike on both sides, they're close enough for this lesson.) Discuss with the children if the volunteer's face is the same on both sides. Could we put half of John's face together with half of Xavier's face and get a match?

Then, hold the string across the volunteer's face at the nose with the string stretching across from ear to ear. Ask the children if both halves of the face are the same now. Point out that one half of the face has the mouth, chin, and nostrils, and the other half has the forehead, eyes, and eyebrows. Are both halves the same? Explain that it is important where something is divided in order for symmetry to be obtained.

Group the children into pairs. Give each pair a 12-by-18-inch piece of black construction paper and some pattern blocks. Fold the paper in half so that there is a crease down the middle. Open the paper. Have the children build a design with the pattern blocks on the paper, with the crease being the line of symmetry. The children in each pair will have to work closely together, discussing each block as they put it down, so that both sides will be the same. You might have them take turns—one child puts down a block, then the other child puts down the same block.

To make this easier in the beginning, limit the number of blocks the children can use in their designs. Start with six blocks (three on each side) and increase the number as they get the hang of it.

For extra practice, have the children complete worksheet page 44, **Make 'Em Match!** Teach them that a butterfly's wings are perfectly symmetrical to each other.

All Different Shapes and Sizes

Teach the children to visually discriminate different sizes and shapes and predict what will come next in a pattern by using large, medium, and small felt shapes (circles, triangles, squares, and rectangles cut from the same color felt) and a flannelboard. (The use of one color allows children to focus on the two variables of size and shape. Use different colors later when the children are ready for more challenging patterns.)

Show the children ascending and descending sizes of the same shape. Ask for predictions of what will come next. Also show them patterns such as large square, small square, large circle, small circle, large triangle. Ask them what comes next. Challenge the children to come up to the flannelboard and make their own patterns.

Allow some hands-on work. Give each child a small chalkboard, chalk, and an eraser. As you model the pattern, have the children draw it and then draw their predictions of what will come next.

To test the children's memories, build a pattern and then have the children close their eyes as you remove one of the felt pieces. Invite the children to draw on their chalkboards the missing felt shape.

For extra practice, give each child a copy of the worksheet on page 45, **All Different Shapes and Sizes,** on predicting patterns of different sizes of shapes.

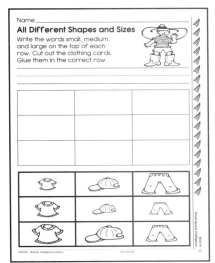

page 45

Musical Intelligence

The Beat of a Different Drummer

Try this! Rather than challenging children to answer math facts in the same old way ("What's 5 plus 4?"), use a tom-tom drum to beat out the question. Say, "What is (beat the drum five times) plus (beat the drum four times)?" Invite the children to clap the answer.

Interpersonal Intelligence

Domino Dilemmas

Have each child work with a partner to create interesting story problems using dominoes as their motivation.

Give each pair a bowl of dominoes, paper, and a pencil. Have the partners take turns choosing a domino. Have them study its configuration of dots. Perhaps one has three dots on the left and two on the right. Have the partners make up an addition or a subtraction problem based on the dots. For example, they might say, "Three gray sharks are swimming in the water, and two great white sharks appear. How many sharks are there now?" Or, "Five fish were swimming in the ocean; then two of them swam off. How many fish were left?" Have the partners write down and solve their equations.

Intrapersonal Intelligence

Journals

Children can keep a separate journal for math in which they can write about interesting things they learned that day. They can write about what was hard or what was easy. Maybe they want to write about how much they loved (or hated!) a certain activity. Writing in their math journal causes them to reflect about their thinking in math.

If children don't have a math journal, you might have them write about math in their regular journals.

Race Against Yourself

When a child feels he or she is ready, challenge him or her with a timed facts test. Give the child a page of addition and subtraction facts that he or she has been working to learn. Have the child complete the page and time him or her. When he or she is finished, note the time it took to complete the page and tell him or her the number of problems done correctly. These become the standards to measure against.

When the child is ready, give him or her the same fact sheet and have him or her race to beat the previous time and increase the number of correct answers. Continue to race when the child feels ready, until he or she has improved the time and gotten 100% correct.

Naturalist Intelligence

Our Animal Neighbors

This activity will increase students' awareness of the environment we all share with animals, as well as the similarities and differences between us and animals. It will also develop thinking skills. If available, read *If Anything Ever Goes Wrong at the Zoo,* by Mary Jean Hendrick (Harcourt Brace Jovanovich, 1993), to your students. The story is about zoo animals who need to borrow a little girl's home one rainy night.

Then make a list on the board of things that various animals and people both need, and things they don't need. For example, both horses and people need water. Fish have to live in water, but humans don't. Birds need to eat bugs, while humans don't. Humans need parents to help raise them, and kittens do too. Make a chart and have your students help illustrate it.

Story Problems

Read each problem. Underline the question. Circle the numbers that tell how many. Write an equation to solve the problem on the first line. Write a sentence that tells the answer on the second line.

1. Sam saw 6 tigers at the zoo. He saw 2 more tigers on TV. How many tigers did Sam see in all?

   _____

   _____

2. There were 7 girls playing jump rope. Then, 3 girls left. How many girls were still playing jump rope?

   _____

   _____

3. Tom ate 4 cookies. Bill ate 5 cookies. How many cookies did they eat in all?

   _____

   _____

4. There were 9 little fish in the sea. A big fish came and ate 8 of them. How many little fish were left?

   _____

   _____

MATH

Verbal-Linguistic Intelligence

One More

Read each set of equations. Write the missing number on each line.

1. If: $2 + 3 = 5$,

   then: $2 + 4 = $ _____.

2. If: $4 + 4 = 8$,

   then: $4 + 5 = $ _____.

3. If: $3 + 6 = 9$,

   then: $3 + 7 = $ _____.

4. If: $2 + 5 = 7$,

   then: $2 + 6 = $ _____.

5. If: $5 + 4 = 9$,

   then: $5 + 5 = $ _____.

6. If: $5 + 2 = 7$,

   then: $5 + $ _____ $= 8$.

7. If: $1 + 5 = 6$,

   then: $1 + $ _____ $= 7$.

8. If: $6 + 3 = 9$,

   then: $6 + 4 = $ _____.

9. If: $4 + 2 = 6$,

   then: $4 + $ _____ $= 7$.

10. If: $3 + 5 = 8$,

   then: $3 + 6 = $ _____.

reproducible

FS23280 · Multiple Intelligences Grade 1

Logical-Mathematical Intelligence

M A T H

"See" What You Count

Fill in the boxes with numbers from 1 to 50. Count by twos and color each box that you land on yellow. Next count by fives and color each box that you land on red. Count by tens and outline each box that you land on in blue.

1									
							18		
						37			
								49	

Make 'Em Match!

Butterfly wings are exactly the same on each side. Draw the other half of each butterfly below. Then color the whole butterfly.

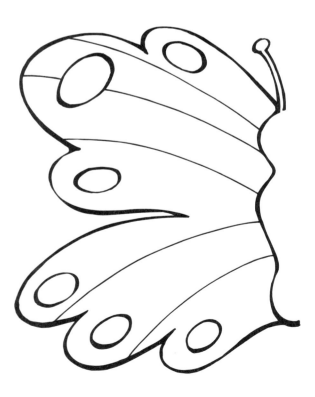

reproducible

MATH

Visual-Spatial Intelligence

Name_____

All Different Shapes and Sizes

Write the words **small**, **medium**, and **large** on the top of each row. Cut out the clothing cards. Glue them in the correct row.

<table>
<tr><td></td><td></td><td></td></tr>
<tr><td></td><td></td><td></td></tr>
<tr><td></td><td></td><td></td></tr>
</table>

Visual-Spatial Intelligence

MATH

Verbal-Linguistic Intelligence

The Life Cycle Circle

Invite the children to read books such as *Butterfly and Caterpillar*, by Barrie Watts (Silver Burdett, 1991), to learn about the life cycle of a butterfly. When they have looked at books and gathered information from pictures, bring them to the class rug for discussion.

Draw a big circle on butcher paper. Make an arrow out of construction paper that measures the radius of the circle. Attach the arrow with a brad to the center of your circle, so it looks like a big clock with one hand. At the top of the circle (12:00), write, *Butterfly lays eggs*. Ask the children what happens next. When the children say, "The eggs hatch," write that at the 3:00 spot on the circle. Continue the discussion. When the children get to the part about a chrysalis, write, *The chrysalis forms*, at the 6:00 spot on the circle. Continue the discussion, and at the 9:00 spot of the circle, write, *The butterfly hatches out of the chrysalis*.

Sweep the arrow around the circle, rereading the stages of the cycle. The next step is to fill in the gaps between the four points on the circle. Encourage the children to give details. Where does the butterfly lay her eggs? What do they look like? Write their answers between the 12:00 space and the 3:00 space on the circle. Ask the children, "What do the caterpillars eat? What do you know about their skins? What do butterflies do after they hatch?" etc. Continue to record what the children know. If at any time the children can't fill in an area, pull out the books and magazines that you have on butterflies and encourage more whole group or small group research until the circle is filled up. When the children understand the life cycle of a butterfly, have them complete page 54, the **Caterpillar Book** worksheet, to show what they know.

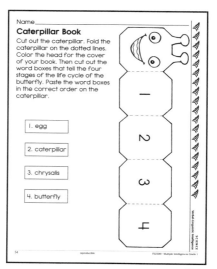

page 54

Places on Earth

Label four large pieces of tag board with *The Plains*, *The Forest*, *The Ocean* and *The Desert*. Have the children help you gather pictures of these places from magazines, postcards, etc. Each time you or a child brings in a picture, discuss with the class what place on earth it represents. Tape the picture to the appropriate tag board. Have the children describe the picture to you.

Write down their descriptions next to the picture on the tag board.

Also invite the children to bring pictures of animals that can be found in these four areas. Describe the animals on the tag board, including information on teeth, claws, mammal or reptile, what type of food the animal eats, etc.

The class may also bring in information on people from these areas. How do they dress? What do they eat? What do they do for a living?

As you teach your curriculum throughout the year, check these charts. Can you add anything to them? The point of these charts is for the children to see the connection between living things and the places in which they live. Encourage questions like "Why does a bear have sharp claws?" The children might say, "He has sharp claws so that he can climb trees, spear fish, dig for small animals, and protect himself from other bears." These charts are meant to build "mind bridges" to help children make connections as their year of learning goes on.

Logical-Mathematical Intelligence

Living Things/Non-Living Things

Talk to the children about the differences between living and non-living things. Teach the children that living things need food, water, and air to live. Do the following experiment to find out what happens when living things don't get what they need.

Plant seven lima bean seeds in seven different cups. Label the cups as follows:

Cup #1—Food, Water, and Air

Cup #2—Food and Water Only

Cup #3—Food and Air Only

Cup #4—Food Only

Cup #5—Water and Air Only

Cup #6—Water Only

Cup #7—Air Only

Teach the children that plants get food from the soil, but they also make food from sunlight (photosynthesis). Give each plant the same start by planting the seeds in potting soil. Give plant #1 the good life—sunshine, water, and air. Give plant #2 sunshine and water, but keep it in a plastic baggy. Give plant #3 sunlight and air, but no water. Give plant #4 sunshine, but keep it in a plastic baggy with no water. Give plant #5 water and air, but no sunlight. Give plant #6 water, but keep it in a plastic baggy and give it no sunlight. Give plant #7 air, but no sunshine and no water.

Have the children help you figure out where in the room the plants can go in order to perform the experiment. Assign seven children to be "plant managers," one for each plant. These children are in charge of giving each plant what is required for the experiment.

Make a large chart titled "Plant Progress," and have the children as a whole report what is happening to each plant. Write the information down on the chart twice a week. Children will begin to prove and conclude that living things need food, water, and air! They can write about what they learned in their journals, or they can keep a science log to record the information noted on the Plant Progress chart.

Magnetic Attraction

Once children have learned that magnets attract only objects that contain iron or steel, have them become "Magnet Machines!" Their job is to first collect all sorts of objects from home and school. Keep them in a big box. During center time, sort the objects into two categories: Magnets Attract Me and Magnets Do Not Attract Me. The kids can sort them into two circular, plastic hoops placed on the rug. Have plenty of magnets handy so that they can prove their assertions. Have the children complete the **Magnetic Attraction** worksheet on page 55 as a follow-up activity.

page 55

Bodily-Kinesthetic Intelligence

Just Like Frosty

Teach children that water freezes at 32 degrees Fahrenheit or 0 degrees Celsius by making ice cubes made from a flavored packaged drink mixed with water. Tell children that the freezer part of the refrigerator must be the right temperature for the water to turn into ice.

While the cubes are freezing, play "Just Like Frosty." Play some music. While the music plays, invite the children to dance around town, just like Frosty the Snowman. Tell the children that when the music stops, they must melt slowly down to the ground and collapse in a heap. When the music starts, they freeze up into solid little snow people and dance around again.

When the ice has frozen solid, pop each frozen, flavored cube into a paper cup and let the children slurp away!

Does Your Nose Know?

Gather nine plastic film canisters. Wash the canisters thoroughly in hot, soapy water to remove the chemical smell. Into each canister place a cotton ball that has been dabbed with one of the following: vanilla flavoring, vinegar, pickle juice, toothpaste, chocolate syrup, mustard, ketchup, perfume, and coffee. Create a smelling center. Number each canister. Have the children sniff each one and decide what the scent is. Write the name of each mystery scent on an index card and number the card with the number of its matching canister so that children can check their guesses.

Erosion

Read *The Sun, the Wind, and the Rain,* by Lisa W. Peters (Henry Holt, 1990). Have the students study rocks and sand. How do they compare? With the help of magnifying glasses, the children may discover that sand is little, tiny rocks. Ask them to guess how they got so small. Then introduce the concept of erosion, the gradual wearing away or deterioration of something.

Set up an experiment where the children can learn how rocks become sand. Fill a big container with a pile of rocks and sand. Have the children make a mountain with the rocks and sand. Ask a few children to blow on the mountain as hard as they can. (Have them all face the same direction, and keep the other children away.) Have the children discuss what happened. Elicit discussion that relates the blowing of air to the wind outside.

Next, fill a watering can with water. Have the children pour water over the mountain. Have them discuss what happens to the mountain. Have a few children take turns dropping a rock onto a rock—relate this to waves picking up rocks and dashing them against other rocks. Have a few other children rub rocks with sandpaper. Teach the children that over millions of years this constant barrage of moving water and blowing wind has caused (and continues to cause) the breakdown of mountains and rocks into sand— erosion!

 Visual-Spatial Intelligence

Petal Power

Read *The Reason for a Flower,* by Ruth Heller (Putnam, 1983). Hang up a poster of a flower, such as Georgia O'Keeffe's "Red Poppy," and scrutinize and discuss it. Have the children collect flowers and spread them all over the tables. Have many magnifying glasses available and allow the children time to look at the flowers closely. Allow them to take them apart and look at each piece. Have them identify the parts of a flower: the petal, leaf, and the stem.

Next, give each child a piece of 9" x 12" white construction paper. Ask each child to choose a flower. With a black, permanent, fine-line marker, have each child draw the flower (nice and big!). Tell the children to pay close attention to detail and draw what they see. Next, allow the children to paint their pictures with watercolor paints and display them in the classroom.

Wild Windows

During a study of animals of the zoo, forest, jungle, ocean, etc., play this game. Have the children imagine they are on a bus, airplane, submarine, or whatever is appropriate for your locale, and they are looking out the window. They see a wild animal; however, they don't see the whole animal, just a part of it. Their job is to guess what animal it is by studying its color, pattern, texture, etc.

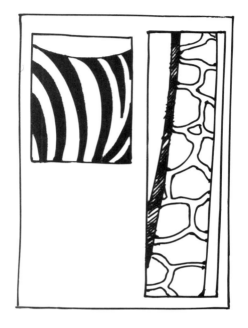

To create these windows, gather magazine pictures of the animals you're studying. Target the area on each picture you want the children to see. Use a piece of 9" x 12" construction paper, and cut a square or round "window" that fits the area of the animal picture you targeted. Paper clip the construction paper to the magazine paper, which has been glued onto another piece of construction paper to make it more sturdy.

After the children have made their guesses, and you've asked them to explain why, flip up the top piece of construction paper so that the children can discover if they correctly guessed what animal it is.

Musical Intelligence

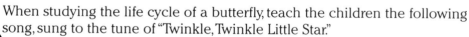

The Butterfly Song

When studying the life cycle of a butterfly, teach the children the following song, sung to the tune of "Twinkle, Twinkle Little Star."

> Caterpillar creeps and crawls,
>
> Eating leaves till it is full.
>
> Then it forms a chrysalis, which
>
> Hangs down from a little twig,
>
> Then one day just look, you'll spy
>
> A brand-new, lovely butterfly.

Give each child a copy of the song, and have them put it in their poetry journal and illustrate it. Or make a big book by writing each line on a separate page. Have the children illustrate the pages. Then hang it in your classroom for the children to read and sing.

Wind

Read about the wind in *Weather Words and What They Mean,* by Gail Gibbons (Holiday, 1990). Discuss the wind. Wind, the movement of air across the earth's surface, is used by mankind as a source of power to turn windmills, which grind grain or pump water. Ask the children how wind helps us get from one place to another. Discuss the use of sailboats, parachutes, hot air balloons, etc. Ask the children how we can play with the wind. Discuss kites, pinwheels, and wind instruments.

Wind instruments, such as the flute, tuba, or trumpet, are musical instruments played by blowing air through them. Have the children help you gather wind instruments, such as whistles, party blowers, kazoos, harmonicas, and recorders. You may even bring in a wind chime that someone can blow on. Create a cacophony of sound, and celebrate wind by using the instruments to play a well-known tune, such as "If You're Happy and You Know It."

Interpersonal Intelligence

Facts in 3-D

After studying a unit such as Ocean Animals, the children can work with a partner to display what they learned. They can do this by making 3-D critters, with the facts that they've learned about the animals written on them.

For example, if two children really enjoyed learning about whales, they can make a stuffed whale. Using a large piece of butcher paper that has been folded in half, have the children draw the outline of a whale. Then have them cut the shape out of both pieces of paper and staple around it, leaving about a foot unstapled. Then instruct the children to sponge paint the paper with tempera paint. After it dries, have the children use a black marker to write facts that they've learned about whales on the paper whale. (Have the children write the facts on a piece of paper first and copy their edited sentences or phrases onto the whale.) Then have the children stuff the whale with crumpled newspaper and finish stapling it. Help them punch holes in the top seam and string yarn through the holes to hang the critter up in the room.

Mystery Box

When teaching a unit on the five senses, invite the children to explore the sense of touch by making a "mystery box."

You'll need a large cardboard box with a lid, such as one that copy paper comes in. With a utility knife, cut a round hole in one side of the box, large enough for a child's hand to fit in. On the opposite side, cut a large rectangle.

Use a hot glue gun to glue a piece of felt over part of the round hole to act as a flap. Have the children collect objects to put in the mystery box. To play, one child puts his or her hand in the round hole and holds up an object so that his or her partner can see the object through the rectangle on the other side. The first child tries to guess the object by using his or her sense of touch. If he or she can't figure out what the object is, the partner can give clues, such as what it does or what it is used for. Once he or she guesses correctly, someone else gets a turn.

Intrapersonal Intelligence

My World

Give each child a plastic hoop or a long piece of yarn with which to make a circle. Have him or her take a piece of paper, a pencil, a clipboard, and a magnifying glass outside to a grassy area. The children's job is to explore their worlds. Have them put the plastic hoops down or make circles of yarn on the grass to create their own little worlds. The children need to examine what they see in their individual circles. Have them draw pictures or write words that tell and describe what they find. Allow the children to dig up a little of the grass, so that they can look in the dirt. Hopefully, they'll find some bugs, rocks, roots, worms, and other goodies. Then have the children hop in their circles and include themselves as a part of the worlds they explored. Back in the classroom, have the children compare notes on what they found.

Science Logs

As the children study a science unit, have them keep a log of their learning. Allow them time to reflect on the questions they may have and to think about ways to find the answers to their questions. Give them time to draw pictures of what they've discovered. Use page 56, **My Science Log,** as a master for the logs.

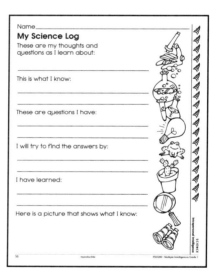

page 56

Naturalist Intelligence

Leaf Collection

In the fall, ask the children to start a leaf collection. The first step is for them to gather four leaves that are different from each other. Have them sort the

leaves by color or by looking carefully at the shapes and the patterns of the veins. Then have each child divide a piece of 12" x 18" construction paper into four parts and glue each leaf at the top of one of the parts. Next, have the children continue to gather leaves and sort them according to the four categories they already made. Instruct them to glue the other leaves in the appropriate places. Have the children give "leaf talks" and tell how they sorted their leaves, and any information about the types of leaves they are, where they found them, etc.

Sorting Seeds/A Center Activity

Ask each child to bring to school a packet of seeds. Dump the seeds into a big bowl. Tape the empty seed packets onto a piece of tag board and display it in the room at the science center. Give each child a spoonful of seeds in a paper cup. Have the children sort the seeds using the seed packet display to help them. Children can sort the seeds into paper cups that have been labeled with the names of the seeds provided and have a picture of the fruit or vegetable the seed will grow into drawn on them.

Once the children have sorted the seeds, have them each make a mini-book. For the mini- books, cut some white paper into halves. Give each child five sheets of paper. On each page, have the child write: This is a _____ seed. It will grow into a _____. Have the children glue a seed onto each page and draw a picture of what the seed will grow into after it's planted. Then instruct the children to staple the pages together and make construction paper covers for their books.

Allow the children to read their books to each other during reading time. The books may also be put into the classroom library with the other nonfiction titles.

If there are extra seeds, allow the children to plant them. Each child may plant his or her favorite variety, keeping a log of the plant's growth. The log could read: *On day one my plant looked like this* (draws the seed). *On day six my plant looked like this* (draws the root and the shoot). Have the children use the information from their logs to write their mini-books.

Caterpillar Book

Cut out the caterpillar. Fold the caterpillar on the dotted lines. Color the head for the cover of your book. Then cut out the word boxes that tell the four stages of the life cycle of the butterfly. Paste the word boxes in the correct order on the caterpillar.

egg

caterpillar

chrysalis

butterfly

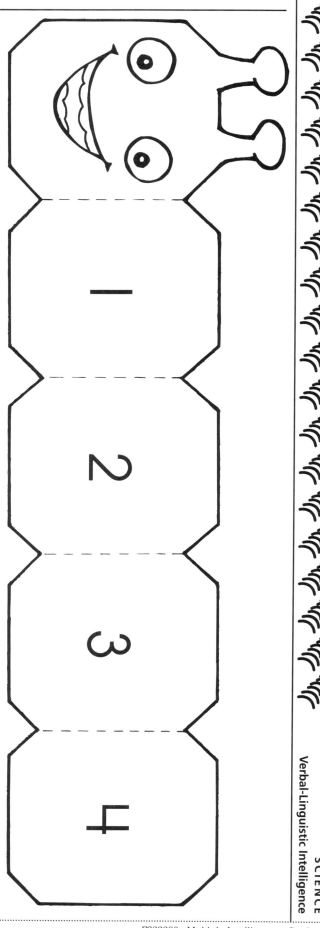

SCIENCE
Verbal-Linguistic Intelligence

Magnetic Attraction

Cut out the objects below. Paste them in the **Attracts** circle if a magnet attracts them. Paste them in the **Does Not Attract** circle if a magnet doesn't attract them.

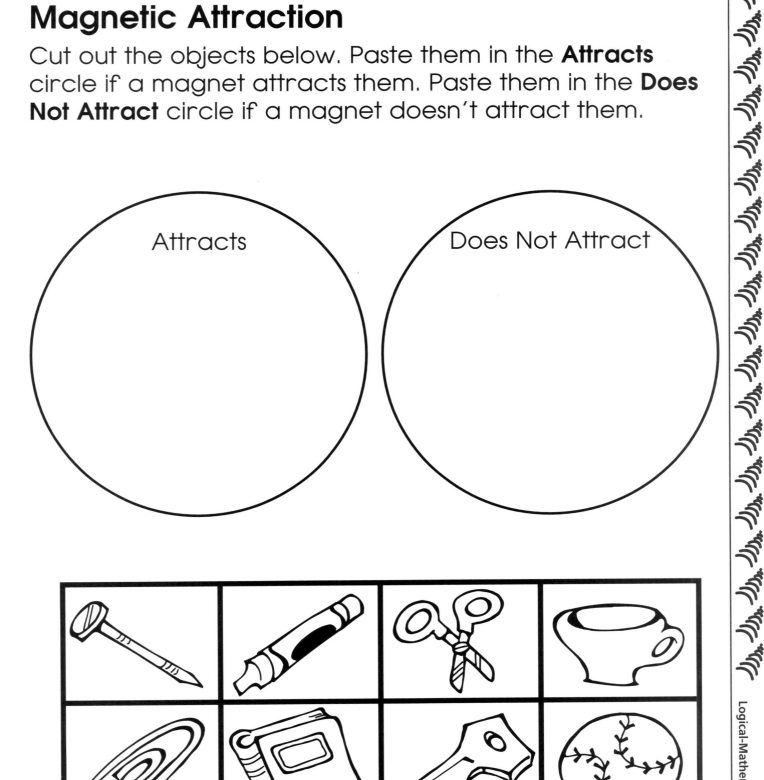

Attracts

Does Not Attract

SCIENCE

Logical-Mathematical Intelligence

My Science Log

These are my thoughts and
questions as I learn about:

_____

This is what I know:

_____

_____

_____

These are questions I have:

_____

_____

_____

I have learned:

_____

_____

_____

Here is a picture that shows what I know:

reproducible FS23280 · Multiple Intelligences Grade 1

SCIENCE Intrapersonal Intelligence

Verbal-Linguistic Intelligence

Song Writing

Whatever the topic you're studying, put the information you want the children to know to music. Choose a well-known tune, such as "Jingle Bells." Make it a class effort and have the children help you with the lyrics. The secret is it doesn't have to rhyme!

Rocks are hard, rocks are soft.

Rocks are smooth and rough.

Some are big and some are small;

They're used in many ways.

We build with them, we polish them

We wear them for jewelry.

At the beach and mountaintop,

Rocks are everywhere.

Circle Stories

For this activity, you'll need to make several "story starters." On index cards, write the beginnings of stories, such as, *Once upon a time a dog named Jake wanted to fly.*

Invite the children to sit in a circle. Hold a stuffed animal. Pull out a story starter and begin to tell a story. Stop at an interesting point. Pass the stuffed animal to the person sitting next to you in the circle. Now that person must continue the story. Keep passing the stuffed animal so everyone gets a chance to make up a part of the story. When the last person in the circle gets the stuffed animal, the story must come to an end. This activity will encourage the children to realize that stories must have a beginning, middle, and end. And it will help to develop fluency. After the children become accustomed to circle stories, invite them to be the first to start the story. They may use the story starters to help them (some may need help reading the story starters), or they may start with their own ideas.

Sample Story Starters:

One day last week a little boy named Johnny found a hundred dollar bill.

A long, long, time ago, there was a Tyrannosaurus Rex who only liked to eat vegetables.

I was walking down the street, and I suddenly discovered I had shrunk to the size of a mouse!

Logical-Mathematical Intelligence

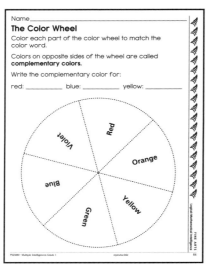

Name_____

The Color Wheel

Color each part of the color wheel to match the color word.

Colors on opposite sides of the wheel are called **complementary colors.**

Write the complementary color for:

red: _____ blue: _____ yellow: _____

page 64

The Wheel of Color

Teach the children about the color wheel. Colors on opposite sides of the wheel are complementary. Have the children complete the coloring activity on **The Color Wheel** worksheet found on page 64. Then invite them to create a design using complementary colors.

To continue your exploration of color, give each child a piece of 9" x 12" white construction paper. Have each child use a black marker to draw a random, squiggly line that intersects with and connects to itself. In the inside parts of the squiggly shapes, have the child paint or use marker to color one color. Then, on the outside of the shape, have them use the complementary color to cover the rest of the page.

Directed Drawing

Teach the children to look at the elements of shape in the world around them. Have them look for dots, circles, curved lines, straight lines, and angled lines. Practice making these shapes on scratch paper. Have the children look at the window in your classroom, the clock, or the bulletin board. Have the children describe what shapes are in their everyday environment.

Choose a picture of an animal that you are studying. Give each child a piece of 9" x 12" white construction paper and a fine line black marker. Tape your piece of paper to the chalkboard. Starting with the nose of the animal, draw the animal on your paper while thinking aloud, "This dog's nose is just a dot. Is it a round dot or an oval?" After you draw the nose, instruct the children to draw the nose. Continue with the eyes, face, etc., drawing each thing, then waiting for the children to draw. Encourage the "no talking while we're drawing" rule.

As you draw, look for the elements of shape in the animal. The beak of an owl is an angled line. The face of an owl and its eyes are circles. Break the picture up into its parts as you draw it, and this will help curb the frustration of children who feel they can't draw. Tell them they can because they can draw dots, circles, lines, etc.

Bodily-Kinesthetic Intelligence

Finger-painting

Most children really enjoy finger-painting. For the children who simply cannot stand getting their hands messy, give them a brush. Allow the children to explore the primary colors—red, blue, and yellow. Squirt a bit of red, blue, and yellow tempera paint onto a paper plate. Tell the children to mix the colors and discover what makes what. Can they find the secret combinations that make new colors? You will hear delighted squeals when they make purple from red and blue, green from blue and yellow, and orange from red and yellow. You will even have some children who will mix it all up and get a brownish-gray color. Once they've mixed the paint with their fingers, let them each use an easel and their fingers to paint with their "new" colors—the paper plate becomes a handy palette!

Turn It Into a Play

Read a story such as "The Gingerbread Man" to the children. There are many different versions of this story; it is fun for children to compare and contrast the characters and the endings of each of the versions.

Children can dramatize this story easily. It helps if they have a prop, such as a mask of the character. Masks can be made from paper plates, cut and colored to be like the head of the character, with a handle made from a tongue depressor taped to the back of the plate with masking tape. Allow the children to choose which characters will be chasing the gingerbread man and which character will eat him up.

Choose one child to be the narrator, who retells the opening scene where the old woman bakes a gingerbread man for her husband. As soon as the gingerbread man hops out of the oven, let the characters take over and ad lib their lines. Have the narrator step in to announce who the gingerbread man will meet next on his journey.

Other classic tales, such as "The Little Red Hen," "The Three Little Pigs," "Goldilocks and the Three Bears," and even Mother Goose nursery rhymes lend themselves quite readily to dramatization, partly because children usually know these stories very well.

Visual-Spatial Intelligence

Create a Van Gogh

Introduce the children to the artist Vincent Van Gogh by showing them pictures of his paintings. Have them study the pictures, noting the brush strokes and the movement created in his works. Elicit comments from the children about the paintings. When looking at *The Starry Night*, ask them how the picture makes them feel.

First grade children can reproduce *The Starry Night*. Give each child a 12" x 18" piece of white construction paper, a 6" x 9" piece of black construction paper, crayons, scissors, glue, and watercolor paints. The teacher should model each step.

First have the children draw the mountain range with a black crayon across the bottom third of the page. Then have them cut out a tree using the black paper. Have them notice the jagged edges. Instruct the children to glue the tree down on the lower left-hand side of the paper and color it with brown, green, and yellow lines. Next, have the children draw the town below with crayons, making small square and triangular buildings to create the sense of distance. Have them draw bushes using lots of curved lines and have them color in the mountains using short, straight lines. (Study *The Starry Night* to see what colors to use.) Then have the children draw the stars (simply small and large dots), the crescent moon, and curved lines around and around them with a yellow crayon. Then show them how to lightly draw two interlocking *S*'s in the middle of the sky to help demonstrate the motion that Van Gogh showed. Finally, have the children paint watercolor over the whole picture using thin blue watercolor to create a crayon-resist.

Art on the Wall

For your next art center, cover a wall with white butcher paper. Give each child a 12" x 18" piece of dark blue construction paper. Have the child fold it in half, then cut out a large rectangle from the folded edge to two inches from the outer edges, thereby creating a rectangular frame. Allow the children to paint or draw anything they want to on the butcher paper wall— their drawings should be about the size of the frames. Then have the children glue their frames around their art on the wall. Have them sign their names with a flourish on their frames.

Color by Code

Have the children color by code to find a mystery picture! Give them a copy of page 65, the **Color by Code** worksheet. Have them color each square according to its symbol. The key is at the top of the page.

Name _____

Color by Code

Color each square by following the code. What is the mystery picture?

Code: yellow = Y   blue = B   green = G   red = R

B	B	B	B	B	B
B	B	B	Y	B	B
B	B	Y	R	Y	B
B	G	B	Y	B	G
B	B	G	G	G	B
B	B	B	G	B	B

page 65

Musical Intelligence

Listen and Draw

As the children listen to the story of "Peter and the Wolf" on the record player, have them draw what they think the characters (or just one character) looks like.

Play Tchaikovsky's "1812 Overture." Have the children express themselves with color on paper at their desks as they show what they hear, using lines and shapes. Be sure to model this with your own colors and paper taped to the chalkboard. For example, as you hear the cannons blast, grab your orange crayon and color hard and fast. When the music is softer, you could gently swirl a soft green crayon around and down.

Walk Like the Animals

Discuss with the children the different ways that animals move. Some animals walk on all four legs. Some animals hop. Some swim using flippers and tails. Some animals fly; some slither. Use a drum or sticks to beat out a rhythm. Tell the children to walk like a bear while you beat the drum: ta-dum, ta-dum, ta-dum. Have them hop like a rabbit while you beat the drum: ta-TA, ta-TA, ta-TA. Have the children move slowly, then quickly; have them wiggle on their tummies like snakes, and fly like birds. Encourage their movements with the drum beat.

Interpersonal Intelligence

Let's Play

Set up a dramatic play center with a flannelboard. Copy characters from stories onto tag board. Color, cut them out, and glue a piece of felt on the back. Let the children work together to recreate known stories and to mix up characters from different stories to create new ones. Invite the children to make their own characters for the flannelboard using the **Flannelboard Figures** worksheet on page 66. Children may want to present their flannelboard creations to the entire class.

page 66

Stars Are Born

Give groups of children a blank tape and a tape recorder. Let them work together to create a tape for the class. They may sing a song that they know, make sound effects for the children to draw to such as in the "Listen and Draw" activity previously described, or play some musical instruments to a tune with which they're familiar. Give them parameters, such as it must be appropriate for all of the class and it can only be a certain number of minutes long, and then let them go to a corner of the room to create. Perhaps a teacher's assistant could take them outside or to the multipurpose room to record, if they need quiet.

Intrapersonal Intelligence

What Do You Think?

Show the children pictures of art work by Norman Rockwell (calendars are a good source of inexpensive art.) Have them respond to the pictures in writing. What do the pictures make the children think about? What questions do they have? Do they want to know what happens next in a given scene? Allow the children time to respond to the art work. They can write if they like the picture or not (for any artist) and why they feel the way they do. Writings can be posted on a bulletin board titled *My Opinion Is Important*. Also encourage the children to tell a story about a given art work or write a story about what might happen next in a given scene.

I Show My Feelings

Gather a variety of photographs or drawings that show human emotions. Point out that the lines and curves we see in people's faces give us clues about what they feel. A bright smile tells us that the person is feeling happy. A mouth formed into a straight line probably means that the person is mad. A frown means that the person is unhappy or sad. A wide open mouth with arched eyebrows and big round eyes might mean surprise or fright.

Pair up students. Have one partner make a face to show an emotion such as fear, anger, happiness, sadness, or surprise. The partner should guess the emotion. Let the students switch roles after doing several expressions.

Naturalist Intelligence

Budding Artists

Show children many prints of Monet's art. (Calendars are a good source.) Invite children to discuss what colors Monet used to achieve the light and dark aspects of his paintings. Give each child a lap board (it could be a little chalkboard turned over) with a 9-x-12-inch piece of white construction paper attached with tape, a box of watercolors and brush, and a little cup of water. Invite the children to sit around a tree outside and paint what they see from where they see it. Ask them to just listen to the music the tree and the wind create. "No talking, please. Look, listen, and paint!"

Texture Collage

Give students large sheets of thin paper and crayons. Take the class outside and have them make texture rubbings of different colors. Students lay the sheet of paper over textured surfaces, such as tree bark, weathered wood, leaves, brick, or cement, and rub across the sheet with the side of a crayon. Have the students do several rubbings. Make a large collage mural with the rubbings.

Create a Mini-Meadow

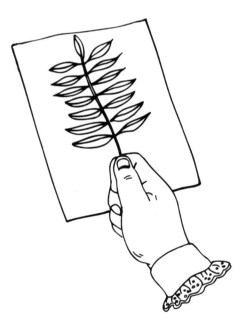

In this activity you will create a small edible "meadow." Obtain alfalfa or clover sprout seeds for growing edible sprouts. You will also need cotton to sprout the seeds in. Create a natural-looking setting for your sprout meadow with clay. With your class, make trees, flowers, shrubs, a fence, a scarecrow, etc. Real rocks and twigs can also be used.

Spread the cotton across a large, flat baking tin. Dampen the cotton by spraying it with water. Sprinkle the seeds onto the cotton. Surround the area with your setting.

Place the mini-meadow in a sunny window. Make sure the seeds do not dry out. When they have formed small leaves and obtained a length of 1 to 2 inches, "harvest" the sprouts. Add them to a tossed salad or egg salad served on crackers and enjoy with your class.

The Color Wheel

Color each part of the color wheel to match the color word.

Colors on opposite sides of the wheel are called **complementary colors.**

Write the complementary color for:

red: _____   blue: _____   yellow: _____

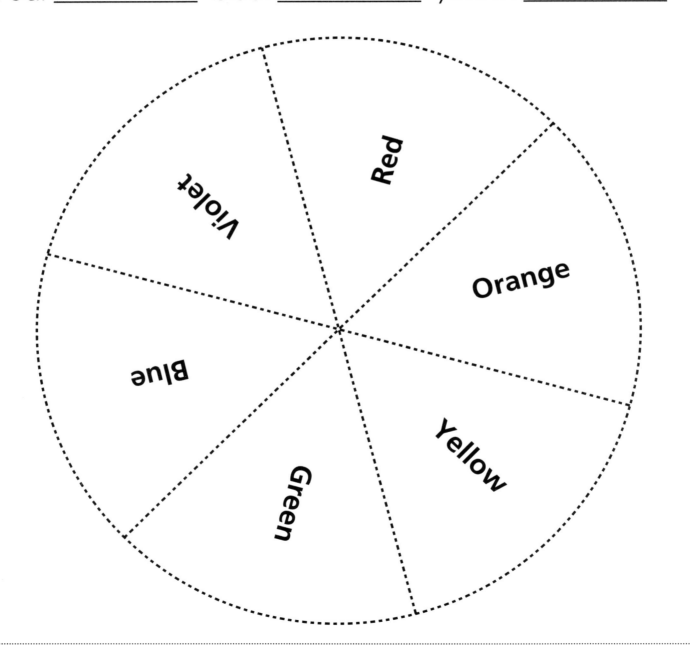

FINE ARTS   Logical-Mathematical Intelligence

Color by Code

Color each square by following the code. Can you discover the mystery picture?

Code: Y = yellow   B = blue   R = red   G = green

B	B	B	B	B	B	B
B	B	B	Y	B	B	B
B	B	Y	R	Y	B	B
B	G	B	Y	B	G	B
B	B	G	G	G	B	B
B	B	B	G	B	B	B
B	B	B	B	B	B	B

reproducible

FINE ARTS

Visual-Spatial Intelligence

Flannelboard Figures

Color each figure. Cut out the shape and glue it to a piece of tag board. When the glue is dry, cut out the shape again. Glue a piece of felt on the back of each shape.

FINE ARTS
Interpersonal Intelligence

reproducible FS23280 · Multiple Intelligences Grade 1

Verbal-Linguistic Intelligence

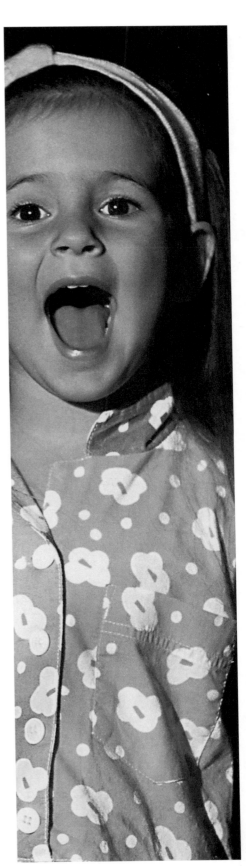

A Balanced Meal

After learning about food groups and balanced meals, have the children create a healthy meal using pictures cut out from magazines. Have the children glue the pictures onto paper plates. Each child can present his or her meal to the class, explaining how it is a balanced meal. You can staple the plates to a bulletin board titled *Food for Thought—Balanced Meals Keep You Healthy.*

Oh, Where Has My Little Friend Gone?

Invite the children to sit in a circle. Choose one child to be "It." Instruct this child to walk around the circle behind the other children and sing, (to the tune of "Oh Where, Oh Where, Has My Little Dog Gone") "Oh where, oh where, has my little friend gone? Oh where, oh where, can she be? With her (describes one of the children) hair so black, and her dress so pink, and her shoes so white with pink bows?"

The children in the circle should be listening intently to see if they are the one being described. The child who fits the description should hop up and chase the child who is "It" around the circle. If "It" can run to where the friend was sitting and sit down, he or she is safe and gets to be "It" again. If the second child tags "It," then "It" has to go to the "mush pot," or the middle of the circle. Then the second child becomes "It," and the game begins again.

Shoot to Spell

Have several players gather around a basketball hoop with one basketball, a mini-chalkboard, and a piece of chalk. Their job is to work together to spell a word. It can be a spelling word or a vocabulary word from a unit they are studying. Provide the children with a list of words to use. To spell the word, the children must "earn" the letters. To earn a letter, the players must make a basket. The players take turns shooting the ball. When one of them makes a basket, he or she writes the first letter of the word on the chalkboard. Play continues until all the letters have been earned and the word is spelled. All the players win! Then have the children choose a new word, and play resumes.

Logical-Mathematical Intelligence

Target Practice

The object of this game is to see which team can reach 30 points first by tossing beanbags into circular plastic hoops that have been given different point values.

Set up two sets of three circular plastic hoops in a vertical row on the blacktop. In the first circular plastic hoop, write the number two on the blacktop with a piece of chalk; in the second, write the number four; and in the third, write the number six.

Divide the class into two teams. Give one person from each team a mini-chalkboard and chalk. They are the scorekeepers, and they should stand at the end of the rows of circular plastic hoops. Designate one person from each team to be the fetcher. Their job is to fetch the beanbags after they are thrown.

Have children from each team take turns tossing a beanbag into the hoops. The goal is to land in the six hoop to earn points more quickly.

Have the scorekeepers write the number of points earned by each toss—two, four, six, or zero. Instruct them to keep a running equation on their chalkboards (Team One: $2 + 6 + 4 + 0 + 0 + 4$). The children and the scorekeepers should be responsible for adding the scores. They must know when they've reached 30 (they should keep a running tab in their heads). If all the children on each team have had a toss and no team has yet reached 30, play continues to progress until 30 is reached. The team that reaches 30 first is declared the winner. Both chalkboards are erased, and a new game begins.

Who Is Gone?

Have the children set up their chairs in a big circle and sit down. Put one chair in the middle of the circle. Choose a child to be "It." Have "It" sit in the chair in the middle of the circle, blindfold him or her, and have him or her cover his or her ears. After this is done, tap another child on the shoulder. That child should disappear behind a bookcase or any hidden spot. While he or she is hiding, have the rest of the children switch places quickly and silently. Then take the blindfold off "It" and ask him or her to name the person who is missing. Give "It" three guesses. If "It" guesses correctly, the hidden child returns to the big circle and "It" gets to choose who will be "It" next. If, after three guesses, "It" doesn't know, have the hidden child come out. That child gets to be "It" and the guessing child returns to the big circle.

Bodily-Kinesthetic Intelligence

The Tightrope Walker

Lay a jump rope on the grass, and pull it straight. Have the children take off their shoes, and, in their stocking feet, walk the tightrope. Their arms should be straight out to help them balance so they don't "fall" off. Children will be able to feel the rope under their feet.

Then instruct the children to walk the tightrope while balancing a beanbag on their heads. This will prevent them from looking down at the rope, and they will focus on the movements of their body more.

Next, have the children walk the tight rope sideways. Try this with and without the beanbags.

Milk Cartons to the Rescue

Gather one-gallon plastic milk cartons—one for each child. Wash them, then cut them horizontally across the middle. Turn the tops upside down and hold them by the handles. Hooray! You now have a "super-scooper" with which to catch old tennis or racquet balls. Children can practice eye-hand coordination by tossing balls to a partner and catching them in their super-scoopers.

Visual-Spatial Intelligence

Obstacle Course Relay

Set up an obstacle course on the grass. Set up four parts to the obstacle course in a rectangular shape. Use orange cones to designate the four areas. Divide the class into two teams. Two children, one from each team, race at a time.

Make a starting point with an orange cone where the two teams line up. Locate the first area about 10 feet away from the starting point. Children must run to the first area.

In the first area, lay down eight circular plastic hoops in pairs. The children must hop right foot, left foot, right foot, left foot, etc., through the hoops, and run to the second area.

In the second area, have a bucket filled with beanbags. Instruct each child to put a beanbag on his or her head and on the back of one hand, and race to the third area.

In the third area, have the children drop the beanbags into another bucket. Then have them each pick up a jump rope and jump 10 times. Then they may drop the ropes and run to the fourth area.

In the fourth area, have the children get on their hands and knees and push a basketball with their heads to the starting point. Then have them tag the next person's hand and go back with their team.

Choose two children to be the "course keepers." These children return the basketballs to the fourth area, and make sure the beanbags get back to the second area before the next runner reaches those areas.

The team that finishes first wins.

Don't Break the Snake

Children have to walk in a line all the time at school. Whether it is going into the classroom, going out for a fire drill, or lining up to go to an assembly, the concept of "single file" must be taught.

A fun way to practice walking in a single file line is to play "Don't Break the Snake." Take the children outdoors. Have them line up in a single file so they are looking at the back of the head of the person in front of them. Announce to them that they are now a snake. Go to the front of the line to be the head of the snake. The last people in line are the tail of the snake. The object of the game is to not break the snake. Begin walking with the children following you. Walk in a circle and in an S-formation. Go faster and faster until you are leading the children on a crazy, zig-zag path, all the while calling out, "Don't break the snake!" The children must be aware of the children in front of them and behind them. You'll hear them saying, "The tail has to go faster! You guys are breaking the snake!"

Remind the children that snakes don't talk, and they don't have hands so they can't touch each other. Playing several sessions of this game will help children walk in a single file line better. A simple reminder of "Don't break the snake" helps them focus on each other and their line when walking somewhere as a class.

Musical Intelligence

Do the Yankee Doodle!

Sing the lyrics below to the tune of "Yankee Doodle," keeping the rhythm with a drum or sticks, and have the children perform what you sing:

All the children stood right up

then they started jumping,

jumped quite high, then jumped so low,

then they started skipping.

All the children skipped around

in a great big circle,

skipped quite fast then they slowed down,

then they started clapping.

All the children clapped their hands,

loudly, then so softly,

clapped until they sat right down,

and folded their hands neatly.

The Body Rap

Teach your children to "rap" and to move to this jazzy poem!

Everybody up and jump, jump, jump. (Children should jump.)

Listen to your heart beat, thump, thump, thump. (Tap your chest.)

Feel your lungs breathe in and out. (Inhale and exhale.)

A healthy body's what it's all about. (Clap to the beat.)

Stretch your arms, way up high. (Stretch arms straight up.)

Now stand on your toes and tickle the sky. (Wiggle fingers.)

Keep your legs straight and touch the ground. (Touch ground.)

S-t-r-e-t-c-h-i-n-g keeps your muscles sound. (Continue touching ground.)

Slowly come up and breathe in and out. (Inhale and exhale.)

A healthy body's what it's all about. (Clap to the beat.)

A healthy body's what it's all about...Yeah! (Give each other a "high five.")

Hula Polka

Set many circular plastic hoops on the floor, all around the room. Have the children stand around the hoops, about three children per hoop. Play the song, "Hokey Pokey." Have the children use the hoops as their circles, rather than the whole class making a circle.

Interpersonal Intelligence

Lean on Me

Children must work with a partner to play this game. Have two children stand back to back (it helps if they are of similar height). Have them hook elbows and lean back against each other. Then instruct them to slowly sit down. The challenge is to stand up again! They must lean on each other to succeed.

Just Like Me

Children play this game in pairs. Have two children face each other. One person is "Me;" the other is "Just Like Me." The person who is Me makes a face. Then the other child makes a face, just like the person who is Me. The person who is Me raises his or her hand and wiggles the fingers. The other child does the same. Tell the children they are imagining they are looking into a mirror. The mirror makes the action as the person looking into the mirror does it. Can they do it? Have the children take turns being "Me" and "Just Like Me."

Line Soccer

Divide the class into two teams. Draw two chalk lines on the blacktop about 25 feet away from each other. Have each team line up on a chalk line facing the other team. Put a soccer ball between the two teams. Make an X to mark the ball's spot. Give each child on each team a number or a letter (you can write them on slips of paper). Use the same numbers or letters for both teams. Call out a number or a letter. (It helps to keep track of the ones you've called by jotting them down on a piece of paper on a clipboard.) The children who have that number or letter run to the ball, and, without using their hands, try to kick the ball through the opposing team's line. The children waiting on the line try to kick the ball back into the field of play. If a child kicks the ball through the line, his team scores a point. The ball must stay on the ground—no "fly" balls.

Charades

On slips of paper, write different physical activities, such as:

Wash the dishes

Sweep the floor

Hoe the garden

Dig a hole

Row a boat

Swim in a pool

Surf on a surfboard

Run a race

Skate on the ice

Climb a tree

Drive a car

Play basketball

Eat a giant sandwich

Act like a monkey (elephant, seal, snake, penguin, etc.)

Invite a child to come up in front of the class and choose a slip of paper. After reading it, have the child act it out, while all the children copy him. Have the children guess what they are doing. The child who guesses first gets to choose and act out the next charade.

Intrapersonal Intelligence

Tune-in to Yourself

After physical activity, or in the middle of a rainy day, invite the children to lie on the carpet and close their eyes. Put on some quiet, classical music. In a gentle voice, tell them to tune-in to themselves. Say:

Relax.

Rest your toes. Rest your feet.

Rest your knees. Rest your legs.

Rest your hips. Rest your back.

Rest your tummy. Rest your shoulders.

Rest your fingers. Rest your arms.

Rest your neck. Rest your head.

Rest your eyes. Rest your mouth.

Rest your tongue. Rest your forehead.

Breathe in deeply. Let the air out slowly.

Let the children relax for a few minutes, simply enjoying the music. When it's time to get up, reverse the process, saying, "Wake your toes. Wake your feet…"

Personal Best

Challenge the children to become more physically fit. Brainstorm with the children things they like to do, such as jump a rope, bounce a ball, or touch their toes. Have them fill in the **My Personal Best** worksheet on page 75, which tells what they can do now (I can jump a rope eight times in row) and what they can do after two weeks (Now I can jump a rope 14 times in a row!). Give them time to really practice, so that they can improve. Enjoy their pride as they fill in the chart with their improved scores.

Naturalist Intelligence

page 75

Dolphin Behavior

This movement activity stimulates students' bodily-kinesthetic intelligence while letting them learn about various dolphin actions and formations. List the actions on the chalkboard. Explain and discuss each. Then invite students to practice the movement on the playground, pretending it is an ocean. You may want to play music selections that are sounds of the sea while doing this activity.

Breaching: Leap completely out of the water; a form of play. Students can leap up out of the "water."

Tail smacking: Slap tail on the water; sometimes done to communicate who is in charge. Students can balance on their hands and then slap their feet on the ground.

Bow riding or surfing: Ride and leap the waves made by boats or large whales; a form of play. Students can pretend to be surfing and then leap.

Dancing: Balance on tail while twisting and turning in the air; a form of play. Students can try to do a full turn while jumping in the air.

Tossing and catching: Toss fish or seaweed back and forth to each other; a form of play or practice for catching food. Students can toss balls to each other while moving.

Chasing: Chase other dolphins; a form of play or practice for catching food, sometimes done to communicate who is in charge. Students can play dolphin tag and chase each other.

Hunting: Form a circle around a school of fish to capture them. Students can move around in a circle and, one by one, dart into the center to feed.

My Personal Best

Write five things that you like to do.
Tell how many times you can do them.
After two weeks of practicing, write
how many times you can do each thing.

Things I Can Do:

1. _____

2. _____

3. _____

4. _____

5. _____

(I practiced!) Now I Can:

1. _____

2. _____

3. _____

4. _____

5. _____

PHYSICAL EDUCATION
Intrapersonal Intelligence

Page 20 Which Way Do I Go?

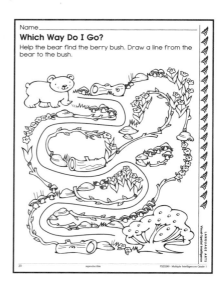

Page 43 "See" What You Count

Page 21 Compound Creations

blueberry, pancake, earring, football, fireman

Page 41 Story Problems

1. 6 + 2 = 8; Sam sees 8 tigers.
2. 7 − 3 = 4; There were 4 girls still playing jump rope.
3. 4 + 5 = 9; They ate 9 cookies in all.
4. 9 − 8 = 1; There was 1 fish left.

Page 42 One More

1. 6	2. 9
3. 10	4. 8
5. 10	6. 3
7. 6	8. 10
9. 3	10. 9

Page 55 Magnetic Attraction

Magnets attract: nail, scissors, paper clip, key
Magnets do not attract: crayon, teacup, book, baseball

Page 64 The Color Wheel

red:green;   blue: orange;   yellow: violet

Page 65 Color by Code

The mystery picture is a flower.